Date Due

Travel and Description Series · Volume X

Per Hagen (Peter Peterson), 1821–1900, and his wife Marie (Mary), 1821–1904, in their home Fredheim in Norway.

On Both Sides
Of The Ocean

A PART OF PER HAGEN'S JOURNEY

TRANSLATED, WITH INTRODUCTION AND NOTES,

by Kate Stafford and Harald Naess

1984

The Norwegian-American Historical Association

NORTHFIELD · MINNESOTA

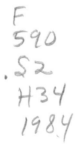

Preface

Volume one of the Travel and Description Series appeared as the first publication of The Norwegian-American Historical Association in late 1926. This series was designed to present in English translation significant documents from the history of Norwegians in America, such as travel accounts, reminiscences, reports, immigrant guidebooks, and letters. These publications provide vivid descriptions of immigrant conditions by contemporary observers and intimate glimpses of the personal lives of early settlers.

On Both Sides of the Ocean, the tenth volume in the series, maintains the original objective while adding a new dimension to the Association's documentary publications. It is a memoir in fictional form, written in a simple and unpretentious style in the early 1890s by one Per Hagen, a pioneer Norwegian immigrant to eastern Wisconsin. Though assuming the format of a historical novel, the narrative has an authentic quality, casting light on social conditions both in Norway and among Norwegian immigrants in America.

It has been a pleasure to prepare for publication this brief tale with its many endearing human attributes. I wish to thank the two authors, Kate Stafford and Harald Naess, for their genial cooperation, and my competent editorial assistant, Mary Hove, for her careful attention to the many demands of the editorial process. Elaine Kringen, the Association's assistant executive secretary, typed the edited manuscript.

ODD S. LOVOLL

ST. OLAF COLLEGE

Contents

On Both Sides of the Ocean

Introduction

THE MANUSCRIPT

In 1976, while she was working at Old World Wisconsin —
an outdoor ethnic museum concentrating on rural culture —
Kate Stafford began investigating the papers of a certain Fritz
William Rasmussen in the Green Bay division of the Wisconsin State Historical Society. Rasmussen was born in Thoneby,
Lolland, Denmark, in 1833, and emigrated to Wisconsin in
1847 with his parents and five siblings. He served in the Civil
War in 1864–1865 and spent the rest of his life at New Denmark in Brown county, Wisconsin, where his parents had settled in 1848 as one of the first Danish families in that part of
the state. The eight boxes of Rasmussen papers contain various historical accounts of the New Denmark settlement, but
most of the material is of a personal nature. Rasmussen was a
compulsive rather than a graceful writer, and six of the eight
boxes contain his diaries — between 450 and 500 in number
— for the years 1858–1911. Among the miscellaneous materials in Box 1, however, is a separate manuscript entitled *En
Del af Per Hagens Vandring* (A Part of Per Hagen's Journey), a
memoir in fictional form written by one Peter Peterson from
Tvedestrand in the early 1890s and telling of the author's
childhood in Norway, his life at sea, his years as a farmer and
prosperous businessman in Brown and Door counties, Wisconsin, and finally his return to Tvedestrand as an old man.
The manuscript consists of 120 octavo-sized pages, each of 20
lines, written in a very clear hand and reasonably free from
orthographic and grammatical mistakes.

The reason this manuscript had found its way into the Rasmussen papers is partly explained in the text. From it one

3

gathers that Peter Peterson had helped the Rasmussen family when they first came to America, and Fritz Rasmussen, the untiring diarist and historian, may later have asked his benefactor — as he did other early settlers — to write down his memoirs and send them to him as a contribution to New Denmark history. The manuscript in the Rasmussen papers is designated as No. 1, indicating that there may have been other copies. A second copy — in pencil and somewhat defective — has been found in Ephraim, Wisconsin, at the home of Mrs. Olive Smith, the granddaughter of Peterson's adopted son, James Hanson. Although written in an artless style, Peter Peterson's account is sufficiently interesting as a historical and literary document to make one wonder whether it had not already been published somewhere. An inquiry was sent to a Tvedestrand newspaper and an answer received from one Solveig Dalen, who happened to live in Peter Peterson's house. She forwarded a Xerox copy of a series of articles published in 1901 in *Tvedestrandsposten*, which were a slightly different version of the text contained in the Rasmussen papers. Manuscript No. 1 forms the basis of the following English translation, while certain complementary passages from the printed version have been added in parentheses. An attempt has been made throughout to keep the simple style of the original text.

THE HISTORICAL DOCUMENT

The manuscript tells the story of a boy, Per Hagen, born to poor crofters near Tvedestrand, Norway, in 1821. Per spent his childhood working on his parents' croft and after confirmation went to sea for some years. His mother's death changed his seafaring plans — he determined instead to marry a local farmer's daughter and settle in a wooded area near his old home. However, Per soon found that he was unable to save enough money to see this dream realized and so decided to emigrate to America. After many adventures in Canada, he gradually worked his way down toward the Great Lakes, where he settled with his Norwegian sweetheart on a small homestead in the forests southeast of Green Bay, Wisconsin. Per later moved north to Ephraim, Door county, where in the course of time he established a flourishing business. A sentimental journey back to Norway finally made him decide to sell his business to his adopted son and move back to Tvedestrand. There he spent his last years, writing his memoirs and corresponding with his family in Ephraim.

Even though the memoir employs the third person rather than the first — the form of fiction or biography rather than autobiography — dates, place-names, and events appear authentic throughout, and this seeming authenticity is supported by parallel accounts in other diaries. The story, then, is history, and is thus of some value for students of nineteenth-century Norway and, particularly, of Scandinavian settlement in America. The inferior position of the *husmann* or crofter comes across strongly — the Hagen people rent their little farm and Per has to herd for the farmer. The herding experience is described, not in the romantic terms of bucolic literature but with all the realism of involuntary outdoor living in a cold and rainy climate. Per's childhood, however, is relatively happy and the barriers of a stratified society are not brought home to him until he thinks of marrying the farmer's daughter and neighbors begin gossiping about the impossibility of a match across the classes. Historians have looked upon Norwegian nineteenth-century history as a political conflict between farmer and civil servant, while the clash between farmer and *husmann*, which was often the background of emigration, has received less attention. In literature, the treatment of the *husmann* has a longer tradition: Bjørnson brings it out in *En glad gutt* (A Happy Boy), and H. A. Foss later in *Husmands Gutten* (The Cotter's Boy), but both accounts are inspired more by the fairy-tale myth of success (*Askeladden*) than by the indignation that animates naturalistic literature. It was not until the *husmann* was replaced by the industrial worker that a more realistic treatment entered literature in the works of Per Sivle, Andreas Haukland, and others. In discussing his childhood and youth in Norway, Per Hagen cannot conceal his resentment when he compares himself to "a stepchild who has been left out in the cold by 'Old Mother Norway'," but mainly he has kept his humility and *husmann* sensitivity, and this accounts for the bittersweet realism of his tale.

Per Hagen's life at sea is more sparingly described, though there are interesting pictures of a very common phenomenon — desertion — as well as of the ruthless middleman who hid the deserters and got them a new job, for an exorbitant fee. Here again it is the colorful or bitter experience that appeals to the writer — his years before the mast on Scandinavian ships, or as a foreigner who cannot understand the commands on a British ship. Typically, his time as an established sailor on the Great Lakes is mentioned only in passing. The account of his emigration contains the usual elements — the long and stormy Atlantic voyage, the travel on canalboats, the sending of pre-paid tickets, the temporary job of cutting cordwood. Again the helplessness of the immigrants is emphasized — newcomers who do not understand the language or are unable to pay for housing and medical care, as in the case of the Rasmussen family.

In the description of the actual settlement, Per's difficulties are not concealed. He speaks of the Norwegian immigrants who expected to see fried pigeons flying into their mouths and roasted pigs with knife and fork in their backs (as in Ditmar Meidell's song about Oleana), but who later understood that there is no more gold on the streets of America than anywhere else in the world.

The picture provided is one of total wilderness, without roads and with giant trees to be felled and burned; however, the account is enlivened by Per's own spirit of adventure, which had once made him want to clear a site in the forest at home. There is a colorful description of the *svedjebruk* — clearing land by burning — and of house-building and furni-ture-making, with sufficient detail to be of some value for the cultural historian. Finally there is the record of Per's estab-lishment as a prosperous businessman after he built a pier to facilitate shipping, and an inventory of various local products.

Interesting information is also contained in the story of his long fight to establish an Evangelical Lutheran Church in

Ephraim. The town had been founded by the Reverend A. M. Iverson and members of his Moravian brotherhood, and the Moravians have maintained a majority there to the present day. Per Hagen's disenchantment with the Moravian congregation could be a result of business competition with Aslak Anderson — also a pier-owner, and a pillar of the Moravian community — but seems rather to be a disagreement with certain practices of the brotherhood and the emotional missionary spirit of A. M. Iverson's Christianity. Per's similar stand against Methodists and Baptists was probably inspired by the Norwegian State Church idea of national unity against sectarianism. On the other hand, Per Hagen was also the practical American, who would not accept patriarchal attitudes: he pays the pastor and demands services accordingly — as reflected in the humorous story of his cheap and efficient American wedding, which would have cost much more if the ceremony had been conducted by a Norwegian. His unwillingness to submit to the authority of the Norwegian Synod, however, also has to do with its strong emphasis on doctrine. Modern readers may find the most attractive aspect of Per Hagen's religion to be its liberal tone. He wanted an ecumenical Scandinavian church that could span the many differences in the congregation and in this he was remarkably ahead of his times. Typically, after Per Hagen left, the next pastor, the Reverend Johannes Olsen, sacrificed the original independence of his Bethany Lutheran Church by having it join first the Augustana Synod and later the United Church.

Throughout his memoir Per Hagen has taken care to present the factual situation with names, dates, and events as accurately as they are available to one who is recalling the past. His sense of the factual is evident particularly in his 1875 letter to a friend in Norway, with a level of informativeness as high as that contained in the letters and other writings of, say, Hans Gasmann or Johan Reiersen. Per Hagen's account, however, has the advantage of combining the useful with the pleasant, of being history with a story.

THE LITERARY AND HUMAN DOCUMENT

One has a feeling when reading great literature that the life described is a lived life, not autobiographical in its every detail, but, as Ibsen said, something *gjennomlevd*, i.e., something lived through at least in the author's imagination. And this feeling of experienced life sometimes gives special quality even to the most naive literary products, just as its total absence makes many an otherwise well-written story uninteresting.

Autobiographical writing in its most general sense has many facets and stages. There is the diary with its random jotting-down of day-to-day facts or impressions. There is the memoir with its recollections of colorful personalities and events. There is the genuine autobiography with its consciousness of self and the motivating forces in one's existence. Fiction combines the colorful incidents of the memoir with the serious autobiography's consciousness of self, and in such a way that incidents are screened and rearranged so as to produce a meaningful whole. In Norwegian-American fiction, authors like Tellef Grundyson and H. A. Foss drew on their own life stories but added the fantastic when reality did not contain enough of it. Peer Strømme, on the other hand, was not tempted to add much to his own life experience, as we can see when we compare his novel *Hvorledes Halvor blev Prest* (How Halvor Became a Minister), from 1893, with his *Erindringer* (Reminiscences) of 1923. The latter method is also Peter Peterson's. He probably had a diary from earlier years to help him with dates and names, and in otherwise sorting out the most colorful events. In addition, he changed the first person into the third and his name Peter Peterson back to the original Per Hagen. Finally he has given the whole account a tentative title, "A Part of Per Hagen's Journey." His choice of title shows the author's attempt to shape his experiences as a string of interesting scenes, with action and primitive dialogue. The story of the lost sheep shows his naive didacticism, while his sentimentality and his resentment are evident when he compares himself to a child left out in the cold by Old Mother Norway.

Otherwise his story is characterized first and foremost by its humor, particularly the first part, which describes Per's and Ole Levorsen's meandering in Canada. The building up of tension and the abrupt anticlimax in the episode with Mr. Chisham shows a good understanding of narrative art: "Scandinavian visitor's surprise at seeing primitive dwelling quarters of presumed wealthy farmer in America" is a frequent topos or type scene in Scandinavian emigrant literature, from Tellef Grundyson to Vilhelm Moberg. There is also the story of how Per and Ole seek work in the country. They are asked if they can mow and answer truthfully that they cannot, with the result that no one hires them. Other incidents are rendered in the style of the picaresque novel, more particularly the brand later known from Knut Hamsun's vagabond books. Per and Ole knock on a door, a beautiful young woman appears, they speak their fanciest language, even with a few French words thrown in for full measure, and are invited into a large room with piano and Brussels carpet, where they are fed. Ole Levorsen is terribly nervous and spills his milk on the floor. Per, however, immediately has a moving true story about Ole's infirmity — "an unfortunate accident in the woods last winter" — and the woman, being a real lady, understands perfectly. (In Hamsun's *En vandrer spiller med sordin* [*On Muted Strings*] from 1909, the vagabonds Pederson and Falkberget meet beautiful Mrs. Falkenberg, greet her in French, and are asked to come in and tune her piano). This kind of humorous scene, with Ole serving as a Sancho Panza, characterizes the early pages of Peterson's book, from which he moves on to a more serious and more constructive stage in his development. His account is still interesting, but the comic elements give way to an adventure narrative, emphasizing either the romantic hardships and rewards of pioneering life in the wilderness, or later the more prosaic vicissitudes of a businessman struggling to establish himself.

Peterson's character delineation is not immediately striking, and it is easy to see missed opportunities here. A professional novelist might have wanted to bring in Per Hagen's competition with Aslak Andersen, a childhood acquaintance who

came to America with Per's future wife, later joined Per in
Ephraim and became not only the richest man in town but a
pillar of its Moravian society. His name is still remembered
while Per's is long forgotten. There is also Andreas Michael
Iverson, the Moravian minister, who was at first Per's friend,
but who later, as can be seen from Iverson's papers, looked
upon Per as his archenemy. Per's oppostion to the Moravian
Church is mentioned in Peterson's text, but not the clash between these two interesting characters — Iverson highly emotional, and Per Hagen essentially the rationalist — which
could have been the raw material of great fiction.

Still, the text does place Per's character in some kind of
relief. His remarkable solicitude toward the Danish Rasmussen family — helping them with their English, getting them
boat passage, looking after the sick and burying the dead
members of the family, finding them a home and work in
Milwaukee, sharing his hard-earned shillings with them, and
finally giving them his house and half his land in New Denmark — this shows the kind of beneficence that might make a
reader suspicious. Is the man simply naive, or is there some
secret self-serving in these acts of generosity? The first
assumption is contradicted not only by his success as a
businessman but by his general sense of irony. On the other
hand, could Per's generosity be seen as a compensation for the
feeling of inferiority from his youth, something like the experience of Hamsun's hero in *Hunger*, who wants to stay
sovereign — remaining always in the position of the giver,
rather than the taker — even though he himself is ridiculously
poor? Rather, Per Hagen seems to have had the conviction —
shown in many scenes throughout the text — that goodness
creates goodness, or, in the context of the fairy tale of his own
life, that a man is partly responsible for his fortune.

In addition, there is Per's strong belief in Providence, a
feeling that he owes his success also to something outside
himself, for which he is grateful. This is seen not only in the
childhood story of the lost sheep, but again when, as an old
man, he sits once more on that rock in the marsh, recounting
the events of his life and thanking God for guiding him. Typi-

cally, on this occasion he quotes the philologist Ivar Aasen, whom he resembles in his humility as well as his tenacity. Actually Peter Peterson harbored a deep secret, never touched upon in his manuscript, the fact that he was not only a crofter's son but an illegitimate child. According to the Dypvåg church register, Astri Olsdatter named as alleged father of her child not her husband Anders Aanonsen but Peter Størdal, a local farmer and sailor who won the Dannebrog Medal for valor during the Napoleonic Wars. With the assistance of his captain he captured or killed six English marines and sailed his ship back to Tvedestrand. Peter Størdal's aggressive spirit must have been matched by Astri Olsdatter's gentleness, making Peter Peterson a more complex character than a simple recounting of his life seems to indicate. Still, between its lines, his story, for all its untutored style, contains a spirituality often lacking in early immigrant literature.

Per Hagen's Story

On the south coast of Norway, up a narrow little valley between two high ridges, lies a little farmstead or croft, which is called Hagen.[1] About eighty years ago an old couple lived there who were left poverty-stricken after the war between England and Denmark from 1807 to 1814. The husband had been captured by the English and imprisoned for seven years, until the war's conclusion in 1814.[2] The wife had to make her living by herself in whatever way she could. She had to sell one piece of furniture after another just in order to obtain a little bread, and so became reduced to a state of the most extreme poverty. On their little patch they could cultivate twelve bushels of potatoes and feed three sheep. As the croft lay high up in the mountains there was view of the sea for many miles around, and one could see several of the inhabited islands and the neighboring farms. The place was poor but nevertheless had a magnificent view and an enchanting natural beauty.

These two old people had a son who was called Per. He always went by the name of Per Hagen.[3] The boy was lively and well built and had blue eyes and light golden hair. He was, however, a peculiar lad. It was not until he was eight years old that he would talk to any strangers. Therefore, people almost thought that the boy was deaf and dumb, but whenever he was alone with his mother he talked as well as anyone.

Then one day Ole the blacksmith came up to the farm, talked to the boy, and even received an answer. He was utterly amazed when he heard that Per could speak. "Perhaps you can also read?" said the smith. "It just might be so," said Per.

Then Ole brought out a New Testament and placed it before the boy. Per read truly and clearly, as if there was nothing the matter with him. It was indeed true that Per could read, for when he was up in the mountains he always had a book along with him. In this way, and with his mother's help, he learned to read. When Per was nine years old he was hired out to strangers as a herdsman, and so he never received any schooling. But as Per always had his books along in the woods, he taught himself. When the time came that he should prepare himself for confirmation, he knew his Bible history and catechism by heart, and when he stood upon the church floor he was able to answer just as well as anyone else. The minister therefore was very satisfied with him, and praised him for his diligent efforts.[4]

From his ninth to his fifteenth year Per worked as a herdsman every summer and often endured a good deal of suffering, as he had to withstand both hunger and cold. It was a pitiful sight to see him in the evenings when he came along with the herd, wet and chilled to the bone, in his tattered rags with the shepherd's bag on his back. (And still Per would play his tunes on the goat horn, at which he was a master.) People don't think about how much such poor boys must endure. It is, however, a consolation to know that it is written, "blessed are they who have carried the cross in their youth," because this sharpens the mind and sets steel in the will, making one more fit to deal with life's struggle than those who have never felt adversity and hardship.

Once in the month of May it came about that it rained all day and was very cold. Per let all of the sheep go up on the ridge, but when he wanted to bring them together, he found only half of them. Per ran up and down the wooded mountainside, but the remaining ones were nowhere to be found. At last he did find one, but it was dead with its throat torn out. Per now knew for sure that wild animals had been in the flock and he believed that half of the sheep had been ripped to death by a lynx. He then sat down on a stone and cried, but tears and laments could not bring the sheep back. The search began again: back and forth in the woods and hills with bare feet on the cold, sharp stones, until he finally became so tired that he couldn't go on any longer. That evening Per came home with only half of the flock of sheep. He was so afraid that he dared not say anything; he also thought he would probably find them the next day.

The next morning, Per went as usual to the woods with the animals. He made forays into the forested mountainsides and ridges, but all was in vain. The sheep were not to be found. Per then sat down in the heather, picked up his book, and began to read. And he came across these words: "Whatever ye shall ask the Father in my name, he shall give it to you." Then Per thought there was still a chance. He went off into a little copse and fell upon his knees and prayed like this: "Dear Father, give me my sheep back, as I have searched for so long now and cannot find them. Now, You may help me for Christ's sake, for it is stated in my book that all which we ask in Jesus' name we shall receive. And now I take You at Your word, for my book certainly cannot lie. So give me the sheep back, for otherwise I dare not go home. Amen." When Per had finished his prayer, he felt unburdened, for he could not doubt that God would indeed hear him. He jumped about quite cheerfully, and as he came to the top of a little mountain peak he saw to his great joy a whole flock of sheep down on the wooded mountainside. Upon closer inspection it appeared that all the sheep were there, with the exception of the one which had been torn to death by the lynx.

After Per was confirmed he went to sea and was signed on a brig from Østre Risøen as a scullery boy.[5] He had to endure many unpleasant experiences at the hands of the brutal seamen and the officers. He received daily both reprimands and whippings, so that he now understood he had gone out into the world. But Per still thought that somehow this kind of life would have to come to an end, for it could not always be so miserable. The following year he got an ordinary seaman's job, and things certainly did improve. After two or three years Per became an able-bodied seaman, and then the worst was indeed over. However, it was not so pleasant to sail from Norway at that time, for the wages were small and the food was poor. In those days — the 1840s — six dollars per month was the wage. But as the boy was rather fun-loving, there wasn't much he could lay aside for the future. True enough, he was not addicted to drink, but nevertheless it seemed that he could not save anything.

In the meantime his mother died when he was twenty-four years old, and after she was placed to rest Per felt that he was alone and forsaken in the world.[6] He couldn't keep the poor little house either, for it was only rented. At this time Per Hagen, like so many young men, thought about finding a girl for himself as a companion for life. And so it was not unusual to meet Per up on the forested mountainsides, wandering through the woods. If anyone asked, "Where is Per off to to-day?" he generally answered that he wanted to go to the mountain lake in order to fish. But as he never had either fishing pole or line with him, people began to be suspicious, and one or another commented that it was a strange type of fishing this fellow Per occupied himself with.

After Per became engaged, the thought occurred to him that he must look around and find himself a home, for it certainly would not do to marry without having a place to keep his wife when he went to sea. It so happened that there was a little marsh nearby, which probably could be turned into arable land if he had had the means, which Per of course did not. Nevertheless, he bargained with the owner of the land about renting the marsh, and this was granted to him.[7] Then Per began to tear down the old house and carry the lumber over to the new place, and there he built something that would serve as a barn. He ordered house lumber from a man nearby, leveled a building site, and set up a lot of stone fences.[8]

Now people began to talk in earnest about Per's engagement. The girl's relatives cried at the top of their lungs that she could be sure both she and her children would end up in the poorhouse, for she could look forward to nothing but poverty and wretchedness. The neighboring wives also expressed their opinions whenever they had their coffee parties. Aase Langneb was of the opinion that Per Hagen ought to be married, as toads are married in the spring. "Yes, now there will be a manor up there in the marsh," said Ane Grimelund. "By God," said Berthe Kota, "he thinks about making something out of the marsh, clearing it up and building a house, but he will never be able to do that, the poor wretch that he is." "Oh, don't say that," said Ingeborg, Sjur's wife, "you don't judge the dog from its coat or the gypsies by their rags. He may well turn out to be a fine fellow, as he is a good-natured lad, neither gadding about nor drinking and already a skilled seaman, so you ought not to be so hasty to judge." "We are not judging," said Aase Langeneb, "but it seems inexcusable to keep a wife in such a wild place and have her sit there alone and hungry when he goes to sea." "Well, that is another matter," Ingeborg felt. "But then you certainly could pay her visits once in a while and help her a little." "Oh, you think so, do you?" scoffed Berthe Kota.[9]

Now it couldn't be denied that when Per overheard what the old women and Mary's relatives had to say about the match, he thought that there was something to it; it probably would be difficult to clear the marsh as well as build a house, pay the landowner, and subsist, all on six *speciedaler* per month. Nor could he count on more than seven months' work a year, at the most, for in local waters one didn't sail in the winter, and the ships were laid up in the fall. Per got hold of a pencil and a piece of board, sat down upon a rock, and began to calculate: salary withheld for my wife at home, four *speciedaler* per month; my earnings which are left over, two *speciedaler* per month. That would probably work out as long as he had earnings, but what would they live off in the winter? Four *speciedaler* per month would not be more than his wife would require for her livelihood, and two *speciedaler* per month would be spent on clothes and various other expenses, so there was nothing left over. How should he then be able to pay for the lumber, and the building of the house, and everything else which was needed?

No, it would not work that way, Per figured; something else must be thought up. He began contemplating the possibility of emigration — getting over to America, working there a few years and sending a ticket to Mary to bring her across, and then beginning the pioneer life over there.[10] Seeing that he could not make a living in Norway, it would be worth the effort to try in America. Still, it was not that simple, for he didn't have any money. But he did believe that it could be done. He went through the woods to the neighboring farm, therefore, to meet Mary and explain to her about his plans and the trip to America. It seemed that it pleased her, and she encouraged Per to go and promised to wait, saying she would be willing to leave in about two years, when he had earned enough so that he could send money or a travel ticket. "For then," she added, "we can be free of all the whining and commotion which I must listen to daily."

Indeed, it is often that poor people must make for foreign countries in order to feed themselves, for in Norway there are so many obstacles in the way that it is nearly impossible for the poor and those of limited means to get ahead. It is not surprising that those who are raised in a rich home, or never have felt any privation or need, can talk and write about "Love of the Fatherland" and sing the praises of Norway's greatness and delightful scenery. On the other hand, one who is destined to be raised in the most extreme poverty, with hardship and adversity, and who has endured both hunger and cold — such a person can not at the same time write about Norway's greatness. For him it seems that he is like a stepchild who has been left out in the cold by "Old Mother Norway." For this reason you can not expect of him any love of the fatherland or any praise of Norway.

Per now heard that a new ship had been built in Arendal which was going to sail to America. He journeyed there and got a job on the same ship; this was in 1846. The ship's name was *Oceana* and it belonged to the firm of Kristian Stefanson in Arendal. In the month of May in the year 1846, the ship left Arendal and went to Gothenburg in Sweden to load up with planks bound for London (and from there for New Orleans). The ship arrived in London on the 1st of July. Per believed that the ship would go to America from England and in that way he'd be able to get across. Then he heard that the ship was supposed to go to the Baltic instead, and load up there to go back to England. Now Per became discouraged, for he realized that in that case it would take a long time to get to America. There was therefore no other choice than to jump ship and see if he could be hired on an English ship which was going to the United States.[11]

He then went to the captain and asked him about receiving some money, as he now had two months' wages coming to him, but he was told that he couldn't get any. The captain was afraid that men would desert, and he believed he could prevent their jumping ship by withholding their wages. Finally Per managed to press him for ten English shillings, and with that capital in his pocket and a little bundle under his arm, he left the ship in broad daylight and wandered along the street. When he had gone a short distance he met the mate, who had been ashore. "Well, where are you going, Per?" he said, and looked at Per a little suspiciously. "Oh, I'm just on my way to a washerwoman," answered Per, and the mate seemed satisfied. After that Per continued his wanderings until he came to a place where there was an entrance into the tunnel which goes under the Thames.[12] Per slipped quietly down, walked through the tunnel, and came up on the other side of the river. As he walked and wandered through the different streets, he came upon a house which looked like a kind of coffeehouse or inn. Per entered and found that a Danish man lived there who was a recruiting agent and in addition welcomed seamen who had jumped ship. Thus far things had gone well. The man let Per know that he could get lodging and a safe hiding place there and promised to obtain work for him soon. (Per stayed with the recruiting agent for three days, and for that time he was charged thirty *kroner*, which was a month's salary.)

Now it happened that the next day a young seaman arrived, by the name of Ole Levorsen, who had also deserted from a ship from Arendal. He also intended to go to America, and so Per and Ole became traveling companions. As neither of them had any money, the recruiting agent made every conceivable effort to get them signed on a ship as quickly as possible, so

that in about four days they were both engaged on a large
English ship from Liverpool which was scheduled to go to
Quebec in Canada and load up with lumber. The ship's name
was *Atlantic*, and it had a crew of thirty-two men. The wages
were two pounds and fifteen shillings, but the recruiting agent
withheld the first month's wages in his own pocket, and neither Per nor Ole ever got a penny of it. On the fourth day after
they had jumped ship, they stood on board the *Atlantic*; but
now their first true hardships began, as both of them were
ignorant of the language and could not understand the commands. It is bad for a seaman when he doesn't understand the
language, for whenever a command was given to someone Per
and Ole had to hold back to see what should be done, and then
follow. This made them appear dull and always behind in
doing things, for a clever seaman never holds back, but wants
rather to be the first to come forward.

Two days after Per had come on board, the ship was ready to
leave its mooring and set sail upon its long voyage. At eight
o'clock in the morning they weighed anchor, and the proud
ship glided down the Thames. Soon the great city was out of
sight. Per felt both happy and melancholy: happy that he now
was secure from the captain's persecution, melancholy about
having left his birthplace and those he held dear. Now he was
out in the wilderness, so to speak, among complete strangers,
for the crew consisted of people of different nations — Irishmen, Englishmen, Welshmen, Spaniards, Swedes, Norwegians, Finns, and Americans. But in the end things went toler-
ably well and after eight weeks of sailing the ship arrived in
Quebec in September (without major mishaps other than
some damage to the rigging. Part of it was swept to sea, and to
get it repaired the crew had to work for twenty-four hours,
night and day, without eating or drinking so much as a drop of
water. During the last three weeks they were badly in need of
water since some of their casks had been broken, and it was
therefore a great joy to get up into the Gulf of Quebec and be
able to drink the water.)

Per and Ole now mulled over the idea of deserting from the
ship and trying to reach the States in order to meet their coun-

trymen there. But first they had to do something about getting money. Per, of course, had his month's wages outstanding but to get them was another matter. He went to the captain and asked for a little money to buy boots, but he received the answer that when the ship was loaded, then he could get the boots, for the captain was afraid that his crew would desert, and for this reason Per received no money from him. Eight days thereafter he tried again to get some money. This time he said that he needed to do some washing and would like to go ashore in order to buy soap. But he was told that he could get soap on board. ("If you get money for soap, you'll go ashore and get drunk and that'll be your washing.") So Per got a little piece of soap, and that was the end of the money question. The next day Per decided to sell his seaman's jacket; he sold it to a Swede, and received one English shilling for it. This sum was the entire amount of cash on hand.

During the night between the 11th and 12th of October, 1846, two men, each with a little bundle under his arm, slipped quietly over the ship's bulwark and down into the ship's boat which they released and rowed to the opposite shore. These two were none other than Per Hagen and Ole Levorsen, who would then attempt the long journey of several hundred miles with the sum of one shilling in their pockets, about 90 *øre* in Norwegian currency. It did not look very promising to go ashore and begin a journey of several hundred miles in a strange land where they were ignorant of its language and institutions. (True enough, they had learned a little English, but in Canada French is spoken, particularly in the country, and the farmers don't understand English.) In addition they would run the risk of being intercepted along the way, conducted back to Quebec and placed under arrest as deserters, and then forced on board the ship again in order to go back to England without receiving any pay. So now there was nothing else to think about but to continue traveling as fast as possible, and by daybreak they had traveled about sixteen miles from Quebec. They were both tired and hungry and felt they could go no longer without food when they caught sight of a pretty house which was located somewhat off the side of the road. They walked towards it, and Per asked the woman for a little something to eat, explaining that they were traveling and seeking work.

The woman was nice to them. She gave them as much butter, bread, and milk as they could eat and drink, and when they were finished they thanked her for her kindness and prepared to travel further. Then the woman said to them that if they were seeking work, they should go in such and such direction, pointing with her hand toward the road. Then she added: "When you follow that road for ten to twelve miles, you will come to a place where there are many houses. Then you will see a large brick house. My brother lives there, and he keeps many workers the entire winter." That, Per and Ole felt, might be all right, though they thought it was a little too close to Quebec. Nevertheless, they wanted to try to get work if possible, for it was no easy matter to starve and beg. They began their journey in the direction the woman had pointed out, and kept on until about four o'clock in the afternoon when, to their surprise, they realized that it was the same place where they had landed with the boat the night before when they deserted from the ship. Now they perceived that they had been fooled; possibly the woman wanted to get them into trouble, and who knows whether her brother might not have been a spy, someone who intercepted seamen who had jumped ship? It didn't make sense to stay there long, so they turned around in great haste and traveled the rest of the day and the entire night without getting anything to eat.

In the morning they came to a little village where Per went into a bakery and bought bread for sixpence. They walked over to a spring and sat down, ate the bread, drank water from the brook, and, feeling refreshed and contented, continued further on their journey. They now went in the same direction the entire day, without eating anything after the breakfast by the spring. Late in the evening they arrived at a little village where they saw a barn by the road. They decided to go in and lie down to rest until morning before continuing on their journey, and they thought they could slip away early so that no one would notice them. But early in the morning a farmhand came into the barn to feed the horses. He had a hay fork in his hand and drove it down into the hay close to Ole. Per lay farther away and therefore was not in so much danger, but fortunately the man took no more hay that time, for had he tried again he could readily have stuck the hay fork through Ole's waist. Then they crept out of the barn and got onto the main road. It was a lovely morning. The sun was already up and the birds chirped in the nearby wood. The village girls came with their milk buckets and sang their French ballads. The smoke from the village chimneys rose up towards the clear sky. It was as if all of nature was in harmony — with the exception of Per and Ole. They wandered silently and sadly along the road.

They became very hungry by midday, for they had not eaten anything since the previous day by the spring. Then Per went into a house and tried to buy bread with the remaining money, but unfortunately his waistcoat pocket was ripped, and the sixpenny piece had disappeared. Now the last ray of hope was gone — that is, if there can be any hope in being in possession of sixpence. It is strange, but when we lose all our earthly property, we always become dejected. ("What do we now do?" asked Ole. Per felt it was best to try out people's hospitality and entered a house where he met a very beautiful French woman. Per behaved as politely as possible and said "man-shie." That was a French word he remembered from the time he had sailed to France. The word was supposed to mean "eat," and it really seemed as if the woman understood him, for she placed bread and milk on the table and made signs to them to sit down and eat. When they had eaten their fill and were about to begin their journey again, Per thought it would be correct to show the woman his appreciation, so he gave her a muslin scarf.) Now it began to rain, the sky was overcast with black clouds, and it appeared a storm was coming up. The rain continued the entire afternoon, and late in the evening Per and Ole came wet and chilled to a little town which is called Liverpool and lies by the St. Lawrence River.[13]

They had to try to get shelter there for the night, for it was impossible to stay outside when they were so wet and chilled. They therefore went into an inn and asked about lodging. Yes, there was certainly no problem, but when they explained that they didn't have any money the innkeeper changed his tune, and they were shown to the door. Then they tried at other places, but the result was the same, so Per said it wouldn't do any longer to say they didn't have any money: they should just let things take their own course — for it was certainly impossible to be outdoors. Then Ole answered, "There seems to be a barn out there in the field, let's go over there and lie down and die — just as well now as later — for there is no other way out, anyway, since I can't go on any more."

Per was of the opinion that they had to try one more time. They then walked into the next inn and asked for lodging. There was no problem. The woman, who saw that they were wet and chilled, said that they should sit down by the hearth, for in the fireplace a merry fire burned away. "Make sure you tell her that we are without any money." said Ole. "The devil we should admit that," exclaimed Per, and so they remained sitting by the fire. Meanwhile the woman came with some dry clothes and said that they could change and hang up their wet things so that they would be dry in the morning. Ole sat off in a corner and mumbled that they were getting into real trouble. But luckily there was no one who understood what Ole was saying over in his corner. Per thought it would be difficult, surely, when the morning came and they were supposed to pay for the night's lodging, but all the same he hoped that a solution could be found by that time.

They put on the dry clothes, got a good evening meal, and began to feel a little self-confident. After the meal was finished and the woman had cleared the table, her husband came with a jug of gin and a deck of cards and sat at the table. There were some Frenchmen at the same inn; these fellows sat down at the table and began to play cards. They urged Per and Ole to play with them — but Ole definitely refused. Per, however, was of an entirely different opinion. Things were beginning to look none too good for them and perhaps the next morning they would be thrown in jail, so Per thought they might as well have a jolly evening. But he did not understand one word of what they said, nor did he understand the game. Even so he sat down with them; but whether he was losing or winning he didn't know. All that he understood was that whenever a game was over, he received a gulp from the jug. Now Ole began to be truly terrified. He said, "It was bad enough that we couldn't pay, but it's worse that, in addition, we are putting ourselves into debt for liquor and risking the possibility of losing a lot of money in the card game. In the morning you will find out." It was a good thing that the people in the house did not understand what Ole said. After they had played a while and the jug was empty, everyone went to bed. Per slept very well that night, but whether it was due to the previous day's exertions or the jug of gin, he didn't know. All the same, he felt somewhat uneasy the next morning after they had breakfast and the time came when they were supposed to pay for the night's lodging. After having made the following plan, he asked Ole to remain sitting quietly inside while he walked out. He said he would be back soon.

Liverpool was a little town which was located on the St. Lawrence River. By the docks several ships were loading up with planks, and Per went down to inspect the ships. By reading the ships' names he noticed that one of them was from Glasgow, and he saw also that it was hiring stevedores. Per then walked back to the inn, and sure enough, there sat Ole in the same corner where Per had left him. Now Per took the little bundle of clothes which they had and gave it to the lady of the house, asking whether she would keep these clothes for them, and telling her that they had traveled for quite a long time and that their money was nearly used up. He told her that they were now going to work down by the dock on board a ship from Glasgow, but would not get meals, and asked her finally whether they could therefore remain and pay for their food and lodging. It appeared that this tale satisfied the woman; she took the bundle, carried it into another room, and said that it could remain there. Meanwhile, Per and Ole prepared to go to work. They went down along the road to the wharf where the ship was docked, but when they came to the nearest crossroad, they ran toward the left as fast as they could, so that soon they were out on the main road.

They now trotted off and believed they were safe, since they were quickly able to run several miles. Then they came to a big bridge and were already out on it when a large man with a wooden leg came out of a little hut and shouted at the top of his lungs that they had to come back and pay twopence. But they were not in possession of such a thing as twopence. They then implored the man to allow them to cross, but it was all in vain. Per then offered him his pocket knife, which was the last thing he owned, and in addition told him about their circumstances, as far as it could be done. It seemed the man took pity on them. He said something to his wife in a language which they didn't understand. The woman then went into the hut and came back with twopence which she gave to Per, who understood the meaning and gave the twopence to the man. He didn't want to keep the knife, but told them it might come in handy some other time, then bade them go in God's name, and said he had been sworn not to allow anyone to pass over the bridge without paying.

They now walked over, thanking the man for the kindness he had shown them, and were well at ease. In the evening they came to a little village which is called St. Nicholas.[14] There they got work at a sawmill, carrying planks. It was hard work, but they wanted to earn a little money, for it was not pleasant to go on begging. They remained at the sawmill for two weeks and each earned ten dollars. Then they sent money to the previously mentioned inn in Liverpool and got their clothes back. (Thus they were assured that the landlady had been duly paid.) Since they were still so close to Quebec, they didn't dare stay there any longer, for they could be intercepted and brought back. They then decided to go on and now that they had some money in their pockets things were indeed easier. They traveled on again for a few days, without anything out of the ordinary taking place.

Finally one day they came to a place where the road divides

in two, and as they were uncertain about which way they should go, they sat down and deliberated on the matter. The decision was to go to the left. After walking about four miles they entered a house in order to find out where the road went. They were told that it went to New Ireland, but there was a large forest and it was twelve miles to the next house.[15] If they hurried, though, they would probably pass through it before it became dark. The forest was said to be full of bears. It was now getting late in the afternoon and the sun was beginning to sink down in the west, but they thought they would get through before dark. They ran as fast as they could. Everyone they met carried a rifle on his shoulder, and this convinced them even more that there were bears in the woods. Around nightfall, they came out of the woods and then onto a plain. There were three or four houses there, located by a large river.

In the house where they got lodging, they encountered an alcoholic schoolteacher. He was an Englishman, and as they now could babble a little English and make themselves understood, he seemed to take a deep interest in them. They told him that they wanted to go to New Ireland and see about getting work there for the winter, and in the spring they would journey down to the States; furthermore that they were seamen and had now deserted twice, and had neither clothes nor money. After having listened to their tale awhile and taken a gulp from his flask, he said: "Lads, don't go to New Ireland. The people are all Irish, and you can't get any work. Everybody is poor there and you will starve to death. Furthermore it is forty miles more with hardly any houses along the way. But I shall give you a good piece of advice. Twelve miles from here up the river lives an important man. His name is Chisham. He has many people working for him and you can get work there for the winter, and whatever you are lacking such as clothes and other necessities you can also get. And if you leave here in the early morning, you will arrive by the time the clock strikes twelve, and then you can get lunch there." From such a story they concluded that the Mr. Chisham referred to was a great landowner or squire. As the "boozer" mentioned that they would arrive by the time the clock struck twelve, they understood this to mean that a clock was mounted on a building in order to call people in from the fields.

They decided to follow the schoolteacher's advice, and the next morning they set out along the road. As it began to draw close to midday, they thought that they would soon get a glimpse of the estate, but no such thing happened. Now and again they came to a little house and a little opening, but for the most part it appeared very desolate, and anyone they asked about Mr. Chisham merely pointed to the road. It was already beginning to get dark, and still they had not reached the manor referred to. Then they went into a house in order to inquire about the road and ask how far it was to Mr. Chisham's. The woman said that it was only half a mile, and she walked across her land in order to set them on the right path. "Now walk," she said, "straight that way. It is just half a mile; then you will come directly to Mr. Chisham's." This was only a little forest path; they gathered that it was not a main road, but concluded that the woman knew better than they. They therefore walked according to her instructions — straight into the dark woods. When they thought they had gone half a mile, they expected to catch a glimpse of the light from the farm, but nothing changed. (Ole felt that they had been fooled and thought they should turn back in time; this was nothing but a dark forest and it might be full of wild animals. Per was of a different opinion. He just couldn't believe the kindly woman wanted to harm them, for what use would that be to her?) As they were walking, they came to a little log cabin which stood in the middle of the road. When they realized that there were people in the hut, they knocked on the door. A voice from inside shouted, "Come in!" They stepped into the hut where a man stood stirring a pot of peas. They asked the man if he knew where Mr. Chisham lived, and if it was a long way to the farm. The man laughed a little under his breath and said, "It certainly isn't, because Mr. Chisham lives right here. But he has not returned from the woods yet."

Here was the "estate" which they had waited and longed to see! In the meantime Mr. Chisham came into the hut with eight men, each with his axe on his shoulder. The hut, or "cabin" as it was called there, was built of large pine logs; between them moss was stuffed, in order to make the cabin tight. The floor was made of split pine logs laid with the round side down. The roof was of the same type, with a square opening in the middle. The fireplace was in the middle of the floor, constructed of small, round logs lined with clay. The smoke went out through the square opening in the roof. There were bunk beds, one above the other, made of small round logs notched together and fixed securely to the wall; the bottoms of the beds were made of split wood upon which balsam branches were laid. Windows were not to be found there and were not necessary, as the large opening in the roof gave sufficient illumination. This, then, was how the "estate" looked.

They signed up for work with Mr. Chisham and got nine dollars per month. Ole was supposed to be a cook, whereas Per was to stay in the woods. The diet was wheat bread, cooked cold pork, and cold water three times a day. (There was a provision that they could have hot tea by paying two dollars a month; but since the salary was so low, they felt they had to make do with cold water.) Then one evening in the month of February it happened that Ole was getting firewood for the hearth and was so unfortunate as to chop his foot rather badly; he was now laid up and not able to cook. After about fourteen days he got gangrene in the wound and was sent to a French woman who "doctored" him awhile. She used ashes and swine fat but he got worse, not better. Mr. Chisham then took Ole home to his farm which was located 150 miles from the log cabin. Per remained at the cabin the entire winter. Pine trees sixty feet long and thirty inches in diameter at the top were cut and hauled out to the river with ten horses.

Late in the month of May when the ice began to thaw in the river, they started to roll the logs directly into the water and then float them down the river for about 150 miles. It was dangerous work to follow the lumber in a canoe, a type of boat which was hewn out of an entire tree. Many times Per believed that his last hour had come, when he had to go out into the violent current in order to release the log jams which had fastened themselves to the large sharp rocks in the river. (During the day they followed the lumber down along the river and at night they pitched camp and built a great fire. The men lay around the fire sleeping. Before they went to rest, however, they held evening prayer, for they were all Catholics with the exception of Per, who usually sat a little distance away from the others. During the service they would kneel in a ring around the fire, and all of them had a string of beads which they handled with their fingers while they uttered some unintelligible words or sounds. It seemed as though the young ones were not all that serious, for if there was a chance to play a trick on the next person during the prayer — for instance by giving him a good blow across the back of his head — it was never passed up. Such a thing could not be paid back during the prayer, but as soon as they had said Amen, they swore like Turks and sometimes jumped at each other. Per thought it was a strange kind of religious service, but he said nothing. He only wished they would get down the river, so that he would be free from it all.)

In the end everything went well and in fourteen days they arrived at the mouth of the river where it ran into the great St. Lawrence. Here the lumber was formed into rafts in order to be hauled by steamship to Quebec. On each raft a house was built of elm bark, which was used as both kitchen and bedroom. When all this was finished, a steamboat came and hauled the rafts down the St. Lawrence River, eighty miles to Quebec. The crew was told not to leave the timber rafts before they got paid, and for this reason Per stayed for three days in the bark house on his raft. On the fourth day he got his pay, which was to be $60. (However, the company had the custom of giving its workers only half the amount in cash, and, for the other half, a three-month promissory note; but since Per intended to travel to the States and not come back again he offered the promissory note to the company in order to get away. He received $15 for the note and so got $45 in all.) Now it was time to look up Ole and prepare to travel to the States; for now it was finally possible. The ship from which they had deserted had long since sailed, so there was nothing to fear in that respect, and in addition, they now had money to pay with, so they wouldn't have to beg.

On account of the misfortune with his foot, Ole got no pay. Per then had to share with him, and gave him half of his earnings. After he had bought some essential clothing, they set out by steamboat to Montreal. From there they went again by steamboat up through Lake Ontario to Louiston, where they arrived in the evening of the third day after leaving Quebec. From Louiston to Buffalo there is a train; but in order to save money, Per and Ole decided to go on foot. However, they had to stay overnight in Louiston and contemplated spending the night in a train car (so that they would not have to pay for a room. As they were sitting rather comfortably in the car, Per remarked to Ole that they had not gone begging for quite some time and that it would be fun to try once again. If they got nothing, it did not matter that much, since they still had some money left over. Ole thought that sounded all right.) Wanting to try the hospitality there in town, they went up to an elegant house and knocked on the door. A woman's voice called "Come in!" They walked into a fine room where there was costly furniture, Brussels carpet over the entire floor, and a piano in a corner. Altogether it spoke of such richness and luxury that Ole became absolutely terrified, and longed to be outside again. Per, on the other hand, was not so disconcerted and asked the lady (a beautiful American) if she would give them something to eat; he said that they were seamen and were on a journey to the States, that their money was used up, and that the next morning they would have to go on foot to Buffalo, since they had no money to buy a ticket.

True enough, this was a little lie, but what doesn't one do under such circumstances? The lady seemed to be very friendly and obliging. She said that she had no cooked food on hand, but if they wanted bread and butter and milk, then they could have as much as they wanted. Per thanked her and said that it would be good enough, even if it was nothing but a piece of dry bread — and that certainly would have been the best, as you will understand when you hear what happened next. The lady then placed fine wheat bread, home-churned butter, and two large bowls, each containing approximately a quart of milk, on the table. Ole had become exceedingly nervous after seeing all the luxury and finery, and could not really relax. The woman said they should sit down at the table and eat as much as they wanted, and they could have more milk if they wished. They sat down at the table and began to eat, but when Ole tried to lift the milk bowl up, his hands trembled so much that he let go of the entire bowl, which crashed against the edge of the table and banged on the floor, with the milk going out all over the carpet.

Ole was beside himself, red all over his face, and wished he could be a hundred miles away. The lady, seeing that he took it so to heart, said it was nothing to be distressed over, filled the bowl again with milk, and placed it on the table. Per then somehow had to make a speech to the woman, and explained that they had traveled the whole day without food, and that, in addition, Ole had been disabled the entire winter, for last fall he had chopped himself in the foot and was still not completely cured. They began to eat again and Per implored Ole for God's sake to hold the bowl securely. After having eaten and thanked the friendly woman for the food, they left the house and walked toward the railroad station, where they went into an empty train car and settled down for the night.

The next morning the journey was supposed to be continued to Buffalo, but as their money was limited, they decided to go on foot instead of buying a train ticket. It was seven miles from Louiston to Niagara, and four miles from there to Buffalo, in all eleven English miles. When they came close to the famous Niagara, Per wished to see the great waterfall but Ole didn't want to at all; he said there were surely just as big waterfalls in Norway, so there was nothing to look at. They could hear the rushing waters of the falls but the whole thing was enveloped in a cloud, so to speak, which is caused by the great volume of water falling down 200 feet. They continued along the road and soon (on July 1, 1847) they reached Buffalo. Now they had arrived in the United States, which they had looked forward to for so long. Buffalo is a large city on Lake Erie; there were so many ships there that the harbor looked like a forest which had burned.

Per and Ole had almost forgotten that they were seamen and they decided to go into the countryside in order to seek work, instead of getting a job at sea. (After walking for a couple of days they came to a farmer and asked for work. The man asked them whether they knew how to mow, but they had to say no. Per had never mowed hay in his life; Ole, though, had taken part in the hay harvest back in Norway and felt he could prob-ably manage the job, but when the man heard they could not mow, he did not want to hire them. And the same thing hap-pened as they walked from one farm to another: since they did not know how to mow they did not get a job. Then Per told Ole they could not go on saying they did not know how to mow, for then they would never get any work. They had better answer yes and let things take their own course. When they came to the next farm they were again asked if they knew how to mow, and they answered yes.

(Early the next morning Per and Ole were sent out into a field of about ten acres, where they were to prove themselves. They began working and kept on until breakfast time; then the man came out to see how they were doing. They had managed to cut only a little piece, and it looked as if the grass had been trodden by a herd of swine. The man was quite taken aback, for he had never seen that kind of mowing before. He asked them to leave immediately. This would never amount to any-thing: indeed, they might spoil the whole field. But Per asked to be allowed to continue until lunch, saying they did not want any pay if things went no better. The reason, he explained, was that they were unacquainted with American equipment. They believed it would be better when they got accustomed to the American scythes. The farmer was persuaded to let them continue until lunch. And it did go better, so that when the man came to see how they were doing, they had cut quite a lot and done it rather nicely, and the farmer seemed satisfied. They worked for a couple of days, but as it was very hot and they had to drink a lot of water) Ole got sick and had to stop working. He lay in the barn, and Per looked after him and gave him food and drink, and at the same time kept working every day.

(When they had been there for two weeks, Per received his pay, which, at thirty-seven cents per day, was four and half dollars. This was all their earnings after two weeks of hard labor. Per got hold of Ole, who had by now almost recovered, and they returned to Buffalo, where they got a job on a schooner at $16 a month. They made a couple of trips on Lake Erie, but Ole soon got sick again and was brought to a hospital ashore. Per took a job on another ship and made a few trips to Sandusky, Cleveland, and some other places.) When he came back to Buffalo, he went to the hospital and asked about Ole, but Ole was not there. They said that he had left there a long time ago, and they did not know what had become of him. Per had to go back and continued to sail with the schooner until the middle of September. Then Per decided to travel farther west, to Milwaukee in the state of Wisconsin, because he had heard that there were many Norwegian settlements in that state.[16] Per then got his pay, left the vessel, and prepared to travel. He had received no word about Ole and didn't know whether he was dead or alive.

At that time there was a Norwegian who lived in Buffalo and ran a small shop where seamen often came to buy tobacco, pipes, and other wares. Per went there in order to buy the essential provisions for his trip, since he was scheduled to leave by steamboat for Milwaukee the next day. As he was sitting there, an old Dane came in. He looked somewhat dejected and depressed, and asked Ole Larson, as the shopkeeper was called, whether he wanted to buy a pipe.[17] Then he brought forth a Danish silver-mounted pipe. Larsen burst out with a roar of laughter and said, "We don't use such pipes here in America, but one like this," and he brought out a little clay pipe. "This type is what we use here, not peasant pipes like yours." The man was somewhat embarrassed at this reception, and said that he thought of selling his pipe in order to get some bread for his wife and children, who were now sitting at the train station.

Per was moved when he heard of the man's circumstances. The man then told him that he had come from Denmark and had paid for the tickets to Milwaukee, but was now without money and provisions, and could not even get his baggage moved from the station to the steamboat because he had no money. Per bought some bread and sausage and salted meat and gave it to the man. Some other Norwegians in the store who saw what Per was doing became rather ashamed and also bought some bread and sausage. When Larsen saw this, he was sorry that he had laughed at the man, and gave something also, so that the Dane received a large pack of provisions. A Norwegian painter by the name of Wold offered to go with the Dane and help him to get his baggage driven from the station to the steamboat. Per reflected afterwards that it was a good thing to show charity and compassion, for it seems to be contagious — once Per had made a beginning they were all willing to help. Per remembered the words which as a shepherd boy he had read in his book: "Blessed are the merciful, for they shall obtain mercy."

The next morning Per went on board the steamboat *Henry Hudson* and bought a passenger ticket to Milwaukee. As he walked down into the steerage section, there sat the Dane with his entire family, three boys and two girls. The smallest child was a little boy of about two years. The man was truly happy when he saw Per and heard that he was also bound for Milwaukee; he thought that now they would be getting a nice traveling companion. There was also an old Norwegian carpenter on board who wanted to go west in order to find his wife who had abandoned him on account of his drinking and brutality. She had gone to her brother who lived on Indian land in Wisconsin.[18] The man's name was Truls Hansen. There was also a Dutch couple who had nine daughters; all were grown-up and the same size, and were — one and all — equally beautiful. They were supposed to go to New Holland, a place which lies between Sheboygan and Manitowoc on Lake Michigan. At nine o'clock in the morning the steamboat departed. Now our Per was traveling again, going farther west to seek his fortune.

The next day the old Dane fell ill and the following day the smallest boy became so sick that the mother thought he would die, for the child had been in poor health for some time. Then, on the morning of the third day, just as the ship was about to land at Cleveland in the state of Ohio, the child died.[19] Because the mother was afraid that they would throw the child in the lake, she said nothing of his death and hid the body in a chest. But as it was impossible to keep the body in this way, Per got the old carpenter to make a little casket, and put the body in it. The next day, when the ship arrived at Newport in the state of Michigan, where it remained for a while in order to load up with coal, Per and the carpenter stole ashore toward evening with the casket, took along a couple of spades, and buried the little fellow on the outskirts of the town. This took place without further ceremony, though Truls was a good enough Christian to read "Our Father" as they lowered the little casket into the hole. They placed some earth on top of the casket, rolled a large log over the whole thing, and the ceremony was over. Meanwhile the ship's bell rang the first time and they all had to get back on board. It was no doubt a punishable act, but Per was not acquainted with the laws of the land at that time. Old Truls, even if he had known the law, certainly didn't bother about it, and furthermore the parents didn't have any money to pay for the burial. Therefore, it was best that it went as it did.

The old Dane continued to be sick. After a few days their provisions were exhausted and Per then had to help them out, even though his own money supply was not great. Per therefore went to the purser on the steamboat and explained to him that there was a Danish family on board who had nothing to live on. In addition, the husband was sick and Per had provided them with food as long as he could. He asked whether there wasn't a possibility that they could get a little help. The ship's purser promised that he would find out whether it might be possible to take up a collection among the cabin passengers. In a little while the purser came and handed over $16 to Per. This was a great help to the impoverished family in their time of trouble and adversity. Per had heard that Americans were a helpful people, and now he had experienced that this really was true.

After a few days (in which the travelers experienced a storm on Lake Michigan) the steamboat arrived at Milwaukee. Per got the Danish family quarters in a lodging house on East Water Street; but as the husband was still sick, the landlady became worried that it might be a contagious disease, and said that they had to leave the house immediately. Luckily there was an alcoholic doctor at the same lodging, and he explained to the landlady that it wasn't a contagious disease at all, but only simple diarrhea, which could be cured in a couple of days. The woman was reassured and let the family stay. The doctor then made a mixture for the sick man. Per thought that it was mostly composed of alcohol, but in the morning the man felt much better. And in a couple of days he was completely restored to health; so the whiskey-doctor was not so bad after all. Now the question was what to do with the family, who were without means and ignorant of the language. Per could see no other way than going to the poorhouse. He walked to town and found a Danish seaman by the name of Henry Johnson; with his help, they got the Danish family installed in the poorhouse, which was located a mile out of town.

Per Hagen now journeyed out into the countryside seeking work, which he found three miles from Milwaukee, where he was hired to chop wood. He received 37½¢ per cord. One cord is eight feet long and four feet high, with a width of four feet across. Food and lodging cost $1.50 per week. In order to maintain even a modest wage, Per had to cut at least two cords a day, which came to 75¢, about three *kroner* a day. When Per had worked there a couple of weeks, he journeyed down to the town and, in order to see how the Danish family was getting along, walked out to the poorhouse. When the woman saw Per, she began to cry and beseeched him to get them away from there, for they were being kept like slaves. She had to scrub and wash the entire day, received little and poor food, and was kept working from early in the morning until late in the evening. If it was ever so simple a hut to live in, she would still be contented. She believed that they could support themselves by doing washing and ironing, for she was willing to work. Per then walked back into town and rented a house with a couple of rooms. He bought a used stove and got it installed, rented a carriage and drove out to the poorhouse where he picked up the entire family and their baggage and brought them into town to the house. (Things went fairly well for them. The man got some work, and his wife did washing and sewing for people; also the two boys found work, one in a stable, the other as a shoemaker's apprentice.) Per bought some provisions which he gave to the woman and then said good-bye, left the town, and traveled out into the countryside to take up work again as a lumberman. During the entire winter Per kept on cutting wood. On Saturdays at noon he journeyed down into town and on Monday mornings he walked back; thus he had only five working days, but still he cut twelve cords each week.

There were some Irishmen nearby who also cut wood and made charcoal. One of them came over to Per to see how things were going with him. "You don't understand how to cut wood," said the Irishman, who was, in fact, young and cocky. "And you can't stack it right either," he said. "In my opinion, I stack it very well," said Per. "See how well the cord is stacked and how the crooked trunks are laid with the bends inward and the ends outward." "Yes, that is just what you are doing wrong. Lay the crooked part out, and the ends in. Then you will see how this increases the measure." "Yes," said Per, "fake it — one could probably do that, but it is not right, for when one is being paid for a cord, then it should be the full measure." "Full measure, surely; that's what I said, you don't understand how to stack wood. How much do you chop in a day?" Per said that he chopped two cords a day. "Phooey," said the Irishman. "I chop five cords every day," he said and laughed. Per thought about this awhile. "Can that dandy chop five cords and I just two? Wouldn't it be fun to try an experiment?" The next day, he went out early and began to work and continued until the late evening. By that time he had produced three-and-a-half cords. It was the most he could manage; but as he later found out, the Irishman had not cut more

than one to one-and-a-half cords a day. Per continued to chop
his twelve cords in five days each week, the entire winter, but
the earnings went mostly to the Danish family — so when the
spring came, he was just as penniless as he had been in the fall
when he began.

Per's intention certainly had been to save money and send it
home to Norway in order to bring Mary over, but the way
things were going it couldn't be done. Nevertheless, Per
thought that the hand which gives nothing receives nothing,
and decided to wait and see. In the spring, a Norwegian captain commanding a little schooner from Michigan came into
Milwaukee. He told Per that he knew Ole Levorsen, that he
was in Chicago and lived well. Per then wrote a letter to Ole,
and told him that he had been in the countryside the entire
winter chopping wood (and that he had spent all his earnings
trying to help a Danish family which had been sent to the
poorhouse). He had now come to Milwaukee in order to take a
job on a boat, the pay being $18 a month for seamen. Per
received an answer from Ole saying that he had had a better
life than chopping wood, which was, after all, something common. No, he had been to two weddings and several balls, he
had promenaded with young girls and gone to the theatre. Per
was somewhat hurt by the tone of the letter but thought there
surely would come a day of reckoning when the landlady
would want her payment for the beer; as he afterwards heard,
Ole was in debt for the entire winter's board.

Per now signed on with a schooner from Milwaukee and
continued to sail until about the middle of August. Then a
Danish family from Langeland and two Norwegian brothers
from Kristiania came to Milwaukee. These people decided to
travel into the countryside in order to buy themselves a farm,
but as they were unfamiliar with the language they asked Per
to come along. Per had also thought about getting himself a
piece of land and building a house, with the intention of having a home to move into when Mary came, and therefore decided to accompany them. And so, on the 15th of August in the
year 1848, they traveled by steamboat a distance of seven

English miles north to Two Rivers to look over the land between the two towns, but they found it low and swampy and
unsuitable for farming. From Two Rivers they then traveled
seven miles up into the country, to a place called Mishicot.
There they stayed a couple of days with a German by the
name of Braach who had quite a nice house and felt that he
was prospering well enough. They now hired a Norwegian
guide who went with them around the area, but they did not
find anything which seemed acceptable for farming. The
country was very hilly and overgrown with great forests, and it
looked as though it might lack water. The Norwegians thought
that the land was good enough, but the Dane didn't like it. He
was of the opinion that better land would be found if they
went farther on. Per, on the other hand, was fed up with the
whole thing; he wanted rather to go back and give up the idea
of farming. But the others did not like that. They wanted to
have Per along to speak the language because they did not
understand one word of English.

The next day they came across an American by the name of
Cooper. He said that if they wanted to find good land which
was suitable for agriculture, they should go about fifteen miles
farther west, and would then very likely find what they de-
sired. He told them that he himself lived there and that the
place was called Cooperstown, named after him as the first
settler. They then decided to follow Mr. Cooper's advice and
hired a man with oxen and wagon who agreed on a certain
price for taking them and their baggage to Cooperstown. Now
Per really got to see pioneer life in America, as they dragged
forward along the terrible roads full of stumps and roots, and
deep swamp holes where the wagon sank down all the way to
the axles and became stuck, so that the oxen with all their
power were unable to pull them out; usually then they had to
lift the wagon out with long poles. Now and then they came
upon a pioneer's home, but it didn't appear very promising
either. It was usually a little piece of cleared field with a cabin
of poor appearance which was built of round logs and chinked
with clay in the joints; a stove pipe was seen in the roof, from
which smoke rose to indicate that it was a human dwelling

after all. These log cabins were surrounded by thick, dark forest, and it was not particularly inviting to think about settling down in such forbidding woods.

Finally, after great effort, the company reached their journey's goal, Cooperstown, in the evening. Here things appeared brighter. There were quite nice farms with comfortable and cozy houses. Three or four French families had established themselves there some years earlier. Mr. Cooper also had a nice house and was a very hospitable man. He invited them to stay there overnight, and said that in the morning he would show them where there was good land to be bought at the government's price, namely $1.25 per acre. The landscape around them seemed less grim. The fields were flat and even, the forest was comprised of maple and beech and some linden and elm. The next day Mr. Cooper went with them about two English miles farther west so they could inspect the land; and when it appeared that the soil was good they decided to settle there. The Dane, Nils Godtfredsen, bought a quarter section, which is one hundred and sixty acres. The two Andersen brothers from Kristiania took one claim of eighty acres and Per likewise took eighty acres. Now the problem was to get the houses built and finished before the winter set in. They began immediately to build Nils Godtfredsen's house, for when it was finished they could all live in it until their own houses were built.

The important thing now was to start in the real American way. First, they cut the timber, maple or beech as it happened to be, and they took care to get the logs as straight as possible. The bark was left on, since they had not time to even think of debarking the lumber. It was then hauled over to the building site by the oxen, and all the neighbors helped with constructing the house, which generally was accomplished in one day. The work proceeds in this way: four of the best axe-men are chosen to be corner men, so that one man is standing at each corner as long as the raising lasts. The others roll up logs as soon as the corner men have placed the first ones, and they work in the following manner: a sharp ridge called a saddle is cut on the lowest log, and it is notched so that the next log can lie securely. The corner men then stand on this log and chop it vertically from both sides so that it fits into the saddle. When both logs are finished, they turn the top one over and let it fall with its groove on top of the sharp saddle, and there it remains in place. If there is a space between, so that it doesn't fit together exactly, this is no cause for concern, for it has to be chinked anyway. One man splits linden wood into suitable sizes, drives it in between the logs and daubs it with clay. Such houses aren't exactly elegant, but they serve the purpose and are cozy and warm enough, even in the coldest wintertime.

When they had finished building the Dane's house they all lived there until they got the other houses built. They went to work building the Andersens' house next, and when that was finished they began working on Per's house. Per built himself a little house, twenty feet long and fourteen feet wide, with a little veranda on the front. When it was finished, he traveled back to Milwaukee to sign on ship again, in order to earn some money. The little money he had had gone for traveling expenses. This building enterprise, which Per and Godtfredsen and the Andersen brothers undertook out in the wilderness in 1848, was the beginning of the large Danish settlement which got the name New Denmark. It is situated in Brown county, Wisconsin, and it now has several hundred inhabitants.[20]

At first, when Per and the others built their houses in the dark forest, not one of them dared leave the place to look around, for fear of getting lost. Whenever one of them left the house or building site he always had to take an axe along in order to mark the trees so that he could find the way back. They then agreed to cut a kind of pathway to the main road, for there was an old military road from Manitowoc to Green Bay, a distance of thirty-six miles. Since the settlement was situated right between the two towns, it was eighteen miles to Green Bay and the same distance to Manitowoc. It is a dreadful job to clear a home in the primeval American forests, especially for those who must begin with empty hands and no capital. This Per discovered when he set out to make himself a home. First the huge trees have to be felled, then one must cut off all twigs and branches, lay them together in piles for burning, and chop the trunks into suitable lengths so that they can be conveyed to one place by oxen and rolled up into tremendous piles. Whenever a suitable piece of land has been cleared in that manner, the piles of lumber are set on fire and they are all burnt up. It is a magnificent sight to see, but it is also strenuous work. Then the ashes are spread over the field, and the land is raked so that all the small twigs and chips are gathered and burnt. In this way, the earth is prepared and can then be planted with corn, potatoes, or whatever one prefers — for the earth is rich and everything grows well without fertilizer. The stumps are left standing and the farmer plants between them until in time they rot, which takes about six to eight years.

Late in the fall of 1848 Per journeyed once again to Cooperstown to clear a parcel of land during the winter. The Danish family followed along, for the idea was that they should have half of his eighty acres on which they could build themselves a house. Per remained there the entire winter, chopped down many trees and cleared some of the land; but when spring came, he had to go back to Milwaukee in order to find employment as a sailor, for now he expected Mary would come and he had to earn some money. When he realized that the Dane would not be able to build a house, he gave him his house, with that half of the land on which the house stood. He said that he himself would build a house on the other forty acres.

(During the first part of the summer he received a letter from Mary. She said she was about to leave for America and would take the ship *The Viking*, sailing from Arendal on June 6th. Per should prepare to meet her in New York, as he had promised. Toward the middle of July Per traveled by steamer to Buffalo and from there by train to Albany, and from Albany again by steamer on the Hudson River to New York. When Per got to New York, however, the ship had not arrived. He waited there for some days, but it was expensive in New York, particularly since he was unable to earn any money. He therefore traveled back to Albany, where he hoped to find work. As he was walking down the street there, Per met a newsboy peddling his papers, and bought a copy from him. By studying the listing of sailings, he saw that *The Viking* had arrived. Now he had to go back to New York, and, sure enough, there he found *The Viking* in the harbor with its Norwegian flag flying. Per went on board and found Mary. There were a number of emigrants on the ship, some going to Illinois, others to Wisconsin. Traveling with Mary were two brothers whom Per knew from Norway.[21] The emigrants now boarded a canalboat which was pulled by a steamship up to Albany and from there by horses along the Erie Canal to Buffalo. It was a long and tiring journey.

(There were some among the young emigrants who believed they were going to have golden days in America — that it would not be necessary to work and that they would be able to live like gentlefolk once they had come across the ocean. But when they saw no fried pigeons flying into their mouths and no roasted pig with knife and fork in its back, as they had been told they would see, they became discouraged and had to take whatever work they could get. And they understood that you don't find gold on the streets in America any more than you do in other parts of the world. In Buffalo the emigrants boarded a ship bound for Milwaukee, where it arrived on August 6, 1849.)

Per and Mary and the two brothers, Halvor and Aslak Andersen from Ulevåg, continued to the state of Michigan, to a sawmill, and remained there until the spring of 1850. Halvor and Aslak stayed on, but Per and Mary went back to Milwaukee where they lived for two months. In August they traveled to Cooperstown. Per now began to build a new house on the other forty acres, and when it was finished, he and Mary moved in. Now was the time to begin to bring order into a new home. It was then that Mary sang the following verse:

> Here within the wood's dark shadows
> Far from home and native land
> We have built ourselves a cabin
> Where in quiet we can live.

They continued through the winter to cut down the forest and clear a part of it, so that in the spring they could plant a patch of corn and potatoes, and in addition sow some oats and garden vegetables. The next year they built a little barn and bought a cow. Things now appeared to be progressing; they also got a little more land cleared so that they could sow and plant more. The year after, they bought a pair of oxen, for it is not possible to farm without the help of oxen when the trees are too large to handle.

The settlers' houses in America are rather primitive. The house which Per and Mary now lived in was built of round logs with the bark left on and was twenty feet long and sixteen feet wide. There was a door in the middle of the side and a window in each gable-end — just one room, with the stove in the middle of the floor and a stovepipe going through the roof. The furniture was also very plain. The chairs were constructed in the following manner: linden blocks were split about eighteen inches long and shaped a little with the axe, then three legs were bored and the chair was finished. The tables were made in the same way, but Per felt that he would like to have things a bit nicer, so he got some pieces of board, planed them a little, placed a sturdy leg under them, and then he had a proper eating table. They had brought along a bedstead and a clock from Michigan, so everything was now in the best of order.

A little about Per and Mary's wedding must also be told. When they came back to Milwaukee from Flat Rock — where Per had been in the forest the entire winter chopping wood and Mary had a room in the manager's house where she sewed for the family — they wanted to get married, for in Flat Rock there was neither sexton nor minister. Per then spoke with a Norwegian minister and asked if he would come and conduct the wedding. Yes, he would certainly come, but only if they sent a horse and carriage after him. Per then asked if he was supposed to have witnesses and how many. The more the better, was the answer. Per thought that if he had to hire a horse and fetch him, and bring him back, it would cost quite a bit, and then there were the many witnesses which the minister talked about. So, Per would rather try the American way. He suggested to Mary that they should walk a little around the town, and after a while they came to a place where there were several churches. At the nearest house Per inquired if a minister lived there. Then they both went inside, and a minister received them very cordially. Per asked him if he would perform the wedding ceremony, and at the same time showed him his certificate. But the minister said he did not require the certificate, for the law was now changed. Per asked if a couple of witnesses were not needed, to which the minister answered that there had to be two witnesses, "but my wife and the hired girl can just as well be witnesses, so that is all that's necessary."

The minister now placed a chair out on the floor, asked Per and Mary to sit down on the sofa, called in his wife and the maid, stood behind the chair, and performed the ceremony, closing with a short prayer. The whole thing required no more than ten minutes. Per paid the minister $2.00 and it appeared that he was well satisfied, as $1.50 was the statutory fee for wedding ceremonies. Per felt that he had done quite well by going to an American minister, for should he have employed the Norwegian, it would have cost at least $5.00 just to rent the horses; and if, on top of that, there had come the many witnesses who had to be provided for, the cost would have gone up to $15 or $20 and the marriage contract would not have been any more valid. So Per felt that the "Yankee style is the best after all."

(Per and Mary continued farming for some time. They built a little barn and bought a cow. After about a year Per sold his little farm to a Dane by the name of Casper Hansen, moved a couple of miles west and bought eighty acres of land, where he built a new house and cleared ten or twelve acres.[22] They now had a couple of oxen, two cows, two heifers, and four or five pigs, so things looked quite good. But it was hard work clearing the land, since it was covered by huge trees which had to be cut and burned before the soil could be tilled and seeded. Per now began wondering whether there might not be a better way of earning money.)

During this time several Danes had arrived, until the settlement numbered twenty to thirty Danish families, besides a number of Norwegians. And so it happened that a Norwegian man came to the settlement. (His wife had taken ill when she was about to have her third child, which was her last, for she did not survive.) He was then a widower with two sons, little lads of six and three years. The man, by the way, was a nice person, but somewhat addicted to drinking. He had to go around to different places to work, so the small boys were much neglected with regard to clothing and cleanliness. Therefore, as Per and Mary had no children, and it appeared they wouldn't have any, they decided to adopt the youngest boy if the father was willing. Per asked the man if he would surrender the little lad to their care and rearing, though on the condition that if he should later regret it, he could at any time have the child back. The man was happy about the offer and willing to let Per and Mary take the little boy. Now Mary went to work making new clothes for the little one, along with washing him and cleansing him of vermin, for he had suffered a long time. The name of the man was Hans Gundersen; the little boy's name was Jens, but after that he was called James Hanson.[23]

(In the meantime Ole Levorsen came up to New Denmark, hoping to meet Per. He was sick and owned nothing, so Per had to feed and look after him the whole winter. By spring he had improved enough that he could work, and he then traveled north to some islands where he found a job as a fisherman.)

In the year 1855 a Norwegian minister by the name of Andreas Michael Iverson came to the Danish settlement.[24] He was a minister in Ephraim and belonged to the Moravian Church. He and a number of other Norwegians had established themselves there in 1854, but on account of the occurrence of early frost and ice they could not get the necessary provisions for winter. The vessel bringing the provisions lay frozen in the ice, six miles from Green Bay. The minister then became worried and moved to the Danish settlement with his entire family, which consisted of a wife, two children, and a maid. As there was no lodging to be had, Per let the minister's family live in his house over the winter because the next spring they would certainly move back to Ephraim. The minister preached each Sunday in the schoolhouse, but as he belonged to the Moravian Church and the Danes were Lutherans and Baptists, relations between them were not what they ought to have been. The Danes now sent a message to the Norwegian Lutheran minister in Manitowoc about coming up to preach. He did in fact come a couple of times in the course of the winter, but that only made matters worse, for the Norwegian Lutheran minister belonged to a contentious party, emphasizing what is called the pure doctrine and opposing every other church party which was not to their liking, even though some of those being attacked surpassed them in moral and Christian conduct.[25]

The minister tried to persuade Per to sell out and move to Ephraim. He explained how much better it was to live by the lake where the opportunities for earning money were much greater than in the dark forest. Per thought there might be something in what the minister said and also believed that he could in one way or another make use of the lake to his advantage. He managed to sell his property and in the autumn of 1856 moved to Ephraim, where he bought a lot and built a house. The next year Per bought a fishing smack and started a freight service and also did some trading, which he kept up for a couple of years. Then he built a store and started a business on land, instead of sailing around with merchandise. (At first everything was on a small scale; he had, of course, received no training in business and did not understand how to buy his wares in the most advantageous manner. Here, then, was a school Per had to go through. He had no credit anywhere, so he had to buy in small quantities and nearly always paid cash. As time passed, however, his business began to prosper.)

Then came the Civil War in 1861 with its problems. Money was devalued and the price of commodities increased to an alarming degree. A barrel of flour which usually cost $4.50 to $5.00 increased by up to 80¢ and all other wares increased proportionately, so whoever had a fairly good inventory on hand made money. Paper money decreased in value and gold went up so much that it took $2.50 in paper to equal $1.00 in gold. Per was kept busy buying forestry products such as telegraph posts, railroad ties, fence posts, and firewood; they were brought to the shore and two barges were employed to load the vessels which lay at anchor a cable length from the beach; a line was used to pull the barges backward and forward. It was an exhausting job, for whenever it was windy and the sea became too high, the loading had to be discontinued, and then several more days would have to be spent loading. Nevertheless, he still managed to handle eighteen to twenty rather large shiploads in this way. Each cargo loading cost about $100, because workmen charged 25¢ an hour; accordingly, through the course of the summer, Per paid out $2,000 for loading.

Now Per began to wonder whether he ought not to give up the whole enterprise, for what he earned in one way he lost in another and it was terrible work loading the ships from the beach. He therefore sold his house and store to a Norwegian by the name of Kristian Knudsen for $300 and moved to Green Bay, where he rented a store and began business. At first things went quite well. He decided to build a house in town, bought a site, and began construction. But he soon suffered the misfortune of having a fire break out in the store, which was next door to his house, and he had to carry out into the street whatever could be moved. The fire brigade arrived with their equipment, sending water in through the windows of the upper floor, so that almost the whole store was filled. The fire fighters saved the house, but the merchandise was destroyed, and whatever was not ruined by water was stolen, so Per suffered a considerable loss. The store burned to the ground. About eight days after this calamity a fire broke out on the other side, this time in a stable. A drunken wretch had stolen in there to sleep and started the fire with his pipe. The firemen brought the fire under control, but Per had once more to bring his wares out into safety on the street, where he could have them moved away if the fire should get out of hand. He did,

however, place watchmen near his goods. They were two Norwegians, one a merchant by the name of Johnson, the other
Pastor Iverson, each armed with an axe handle. This time
nothing was stolen, but Per had learned to respect fires, and
began thinking of leaving town as soon as he saw an opportunity to get away.

(Then, in the fall of 1869, a Dane by the name of Søren
Pedersen came to Green Bay, and since he had a house and a
store in Sturgeon Bay which he wanted to sell, he approached
Per and persuaded him to move there, offering him the house
for $2,500. Per bought the house and paid for it, and in the
winter of 1870 moved to Sturgeon Bay, which is a smaller city,
and began business there. But in 1871 he went back to
Ephraim, bought a piece of land the size of four lots, with a
small house on it, built a store, repaired the house, sold out in
Sturgeon Bay, and moved back to Ephraim, where once again
he set up in business.)

Now Per began speculating about building a wharf where
the ships could dock to take on cargo; in that way he could
avoid using barges, which involved considerable risk. He then
started construction of a wharf built of wood piers filled with
stone. It was 250 feet long; the first 75 feet from land it was 16
feet wide, and beyond this point it was extended to a 50 foot
width, so that two vessels could load simultaneously. The
wharf cost $2,500.[26] Now things went better. Since all the
materials could now be transported to the wharf, the ships
were able to load whether it was stormy or calm. Every year
Per shipped out 3,000 cords of firewood, 8,000 to 10,000 fence
posts, 1,000 telegraph posts, 600 to 700 cords of bark, and
about 2,000 railroad ties; a fee was assessed as wharf rental,
which brought Per $600 to $800 yearly.

The little boy Per had adopted was now fourteen years old.
He had attended public school the entire time, had been confirmed, and possessed good scholastic ability. Per therefore
decided to send him to Milwaukee to a business school so that
he could acquire the necessary preparation for a career in
business. He remained in Milwaukee for three months. After
that he helped Per with the business until he was twenty-one

years old. According to American law, a young man reaches
full legal age at twenty-one. Then he can do whatever he
pleases and go into one or another type of employment without being under the guardianship of his elders. Since James
Hanson's intention was to enter into business, Per gave him
$1,000 in cash for a start. Five English miles north of Ephraim
is a place called Sister Bay, where an Irishman had built a
wharf for the export of lumber. He had also erected a store, but
since the Irishman was not suited for trade, he decided to
lease out both the wharf and the shop. James Hanson now
managed to lease the entire thing on favorable terms. He
moved there and began shipping out lumber products, and in
addition trading in groceries and manufactured goods. He did
very well. (His father Hans Gundersen also moved to Sister
Bay after his oldest son, James' brother, had died of a throat
disease, and he managed to buy a little piece of land and build
a house. He lived alone and supported himself mostly by
hunting and fishing but was still addicted to drink. He was not
uneducated, for, as he said, he had studied to be a schoolmas-
ter under Pastor Lammers in Bamble.[27] His son James was a
teetotaller and did not like it that his father drank, hence there
was a barrier between father and son and they never had any
personal contact.)

James Hanson possessed a special gift for dealing with people of all types, young and old, for he had a cheerful disposi-
tion and was, in addition, helpful to the needy. Best of all, he
was sincere and honest in all his dealings and conduct, and
people appreciated this so much that in a few years his business increased considerably. But whether or not the cause was
James Hanson's prosperity — this is not known — the Irishman gave him three months notice and told him that he would
now take over the business himself, so James had to leave
Sister Bay, where he had run the business for several years
and gathered a great number of genuine friends.

(At this time Per began building another house in Ephraim.
It cost him about $1,500, and as the old house was too small
and was also needed for storage of goods since the business
had now increased considerably, Per and Mary moved into

their new house in the fall of 1874. . . . Because Ephraim is a remote place, far away from the big cities, Per had to keep a large supply of wares in order to satisfy the demand for groceries and dry goods. He stocked hardware, glassware, farming implements, shoes, prefabricated doors and windows, medical supplies of various kinds, besides large quantities of oats and corn used to feed cattle and horses, since most of the farmers were newcomers who had not been able to grow enough grain for this purpose. Thus Per Hagen had to keep a stock worth at least $15,000. He was also elected to various municipal positions. For several years he served as town chairman. He was also justice of the peace, but this office did not appeal to him. There was often quarreling among the farmers, and when he had to arbitrate in these feuds it was impossible to please both parties. The losing side always felt mistreated, and as a result he often lost, at least for a time, some of his best customers. He realized it did not pay to be both a merchant and a justice of the peace and asked not to be reelected. He applied instead to the governor for the position of notary public, which he received. It was much the same kind of office, except that he did not have anything to do with actual court procedure.)

(In the year 1875 Per wrote the following letter to an old friend in Norway who had asked him about conditions in America. . . .

> *Ephraim, Door co., Wisconsin*
> *September 4, 1875*

Dear Friend,

Many thanks for your letter. I see that you and your family live well, and the same can be said of us. You ask me to tell you something about conditions over here, and in particular, in Ephraim. That I would have liked to do, but I feel I am unable to give you a clear picture of overall conditions here. On the other hand, I can try to write a little about Ephraim and its surroundings.

Ephraim was founded in the year 1852, when a Norwegian minister by the name of Andreas Michael Iverson and a few families moved here during the summer and settled down. Since both the minister and those who accompanied him belonged to the Moravian Church, they baptized the place Ephraim, for it is common in the Moravian Church to use biblical names. The place was earlier known as Eagle Harbor. Ephraim is situated on the 44th parallel, and hence it lies a good deal farther south than the place where you live. We are about 300 miles north of Chicago and 80 miles north of Green Bay. The place is situated on a peninsula which is 75 miles long and 30 miles across at its widest and which ends in a point, so that at the narrowest place it is only three miles across. This peninsula separates Lake Michigan from Green Bay, which is an arm of Lake Michigan and stretches right up to the city of Green Bay. Lake Michigan is 400 miles long and 80 miles wide. Green Bay is 90 miles long, and about 30 miles at its widest, becoming narrower as one approaches the town of Green Bay in the southwest. Ephraim possesses a rare natural beauty. On the coast there are steep cliffs, rising vertically from the sea, though not as high as in Norway; still, some of them are two to three hundred feet tall and covered at the top by deciduous woods, which makes them look very beautiful. The soil at the top of these cliffs is arable and the land rather level, so it is not uncommon to see houses on these hills which look as if they are built right out on the edge of the cliffs.

The population is made up of Norwegians, Danes, Swedes, and Germans. The Norwegians live mostly along the coast, the Germans mostly inland where they support themselves by farming. The Norwegians do some farming, but generally they also like to try their hand at fishing. Among the Norwegians, some are from East Norway, others from North Norway, some from Farsund and Lister, and a few from Holt parish. The woods consist of maple, beech, ash, basswood, birch, and oak, and in the low-lying areas, cedar, pine, spruce, and hemlock. This last kind of tree you probably don't know, since it does not grow in Norway. It is a conifer, with needles like those of the spruce, but its bark rather resembles the pine. The bark is used for the tanning of leather and is shipped out in large quantities. The soil is a mixture of loam and sand and is rather rocky. Since it is limestone, the soil is well suited for the raising of wheat, but it is hard to work on account of stumps and rocks, particularly on new land. The soil at first is rich enough without fertilizer, but having been worked for some years, it needs to be fertilized. Admittedly, according to what I have heard, farmers on the great prairies farther to the west have sown wheat for twenty years on the same land without fertilizing and yet the soil has yielded good harvests; but then the soil out there is probably better. The principal occupations here are agriculture, forestry, and fishing. We ship out to the larger cities great quantities of fence posts, railroad ties, telegraph poles, and hemlock bark, as well as maple and beech wood. Some wheat is also shipped from here. Nowadays threshing machines are being used, and farmers travel to town to sell their grain. They receive a good price. Wheat brings $1.25 per bushel; it is paid for in cash.

Ephraim is not a large town. There are at present two stores, a shoemaker, a hotel, a church, and a schoolhouse, and two piers, where ships can dock to take on their cargo. There is also some steamship activity, since steamers normally arrive twice a week. All land has now been bought, so there is nothing left of the government land, which could be bought for $1.25 per acre. Farther west land may also be acquired in accordance with the Homestead Act; in that case a man or woman, whether he or she is single or head of a family, receives 160 acres on condition that the land be improved by building a house and clearing some of the area. When it can be proved that this has been done, owners will in five years receive a title to the land, which they can then use in whatever way they want. The whole expense amounts to $10, the cost of surveying the land. It is toward these areas that the stream of emigration now takes its course. The best of greetings to yourself and your family from your old friend

Per Hagen)

For a long time Per and Mary had thought about undertaking a journey to Norway in order to see old friends and acquaintances again, and in addition, to see the old familiar scenes. Until this time it had not been possible, but as James no longer had his Sister Bay business, surely they ought to be able to get him to care for the business in their absence. They talked to James about it, and as he was willing, it was decided that Per and Mary should take a trip to Norway. In the spring of 1878, in the month of May, they left Ephraim and went by boat to Chicago; from there they went by train to New York, from New York by the steamship *Egypt*, belonging to the English National Line, to Liverpool, then by train to Hull, and from Hull, by the steamship *Angelo*, they arrived at Kristiansand on Pentecost Sunday. And then from Kristiansand they went on the mail steamer *Ekselensen* to Borøen, where a boat lay waiting to take the post and passengers to Tvedestrand. Now, after thirty years' absence, Per and Mary were on old familiar ground and saw the well-remembered places. They were so busy looking around that they did not notice how quickly they entered the fjord, and soon the boat was alongside the Tvedestrand wharf.

It is rather strange to relive one's childhood memories after so long an absence, for great changes can take place in a period of thirty years. Per and Mary realized that this was true when they went back to Norway. They imagined that they would meet friends and acquaintances as in the old days, but most of them were either dead or had moved away; the few that were left were old and unrecognizable. A new generation had grown up which was foreign to them. Per was reminded of Ivar Aasen's poem:

> You come to a farm, which you think you know,
> You look forward to finding the good old village.
> But the neighborhood has changed; what you want won't be found.
> The old folks have vanished, and new ones have arrived.[28]

All the same, they were home. The surroundings were unchanged. The mountains, the lakes, the hills, the heaths — all were familiar and beloved. Memories from childhood and youth attached to every place. Happy childhood days, how beautiful you can be! They remained in Norway for six months and made many acquaintances among the younger generation. They also visited a few places from Kristiania westward to Farsund and Lister. During their stay at home in Norway they lived with Mary's brother Stian A. Nilsen and his wife Gunhild Marie, two old people, who were very accommodating and invited them to live with them as long as they were in Norway.

Per made occasional excursions in the area, especially to the old farmstead Hagen where he first had seen the light of day and had spent the years of his childhood and youth. It cannot be denied that it puts us in a solemn state of mind to see again these old places where as children we have laughed and cried. Although we may have been brought up in poverty and privation, our birthplace is still dear and remembered with wistful affection. Then he had to go to the marsh he had once rented and which he particularly wanted to see. Everything was as in the olden days, except that the building he had erected thirty years before was entirely gone. But the stone fence stood as he had made it. The marsh was the same, though it was more wooded. It was a strange feeling for him to come across these old places, even the same rock where he had sat thirty years before and calculated his income and expenses which he could not get to balance. Much had changed, but the mountains were still the same. And Per remembered the old poem:

> The ancient peaks against the sky
> Will always look the same,
> The same are all its ancient rims
> And all its summits high.
> The town is built by new young men,
> Whose houses stand to fall;
> But the ancient mountain markers
> They stand there just as tall.[29]

Yes, that's the way it was; much had changed, but the old markers stood just as solidly and were the same as in the old days. Friends and acquaintances from one's youthful years were gone — some were dead, others had married and moved

away. Yes, even the old women who had given Per such a bad
name during his engagement days were now dead and gone.
Per sat upon the rock, deeply melancholy, and thought about
times past, about his childhood and youth in Norway, and
about the past thirty years of his manhood in America. He
thought about the many dangers and hardships he had endured over there, and how he was once again at the place
where he had sat and mulled over things so long ago. In his
heart, he thanked God for the Providence which had pre-
served him through so many temptations and dangers, and
which made it possible for him to sit there and contemplate
the old marking stones. Yes, it was a solemn moment for him
to relive these old memories.

The time was now coming when they had to begin thinking
about the return trip. They took leave of their young and old
acquaintances and friends on the third of August, and set out
on their journey. They went to Kristiansand, then on the
steamship *Albion* to Hull, and from there by train to Liverpool, where they remained a couple of days and had a good
opportunity to look around the town. From Liverpool they
went with the White Star Line's steamship *Britannia* to New
York, which took ten days, with heavy seas and contrary winds
the entire time; even so, the ship made 10 knots an hour. On
the 16th of August they arrived in New York; they continued
the trip on the same day to Chicago and remained there for a
few days in order to greet some friends and acquaintances.
From Chicago they went by steamer to Ephraim, where they
arrived safely on the 25th of August. Thus it took twenty-two
days to get from Østeraa to Ephraim. Now Per and Mary were
back home after having completed their long awaited trip to
Norway. Per found the business in good order. James Hanson
had done his best to carry it out satisfactorily.

During the fourteen years Per and Mary had lived in
Ephraim, the population had increased considerably. A great
number of Germans had arrived, as well as many Swedes and
Norwegians, and some Danes and a few Irish and English.
There was in the beginning only one church, the Moravian

Church, which worked with all its might to gather supporters among the Germans and Norwegians as well as among the Swedes and Danes. The Moravians had the custom that when children were baptized, they were recorded as Moravians, and when they were confirmed, they became members of the congregation. Because of this, the Moravian Church got quite a few members and there began to be dissatisfaction among both the Norwegians and the Germans. They thought it was wrong to draw the children into the church in this way; for the adults, it probably was all right, for they certainly had their own free will. With the children it was different, because they were incorporated by subterfuge: if the parents would not allow their children to be baptized in the Moravian Church, then they remained unchristened, and this didn't accord with Lutheran teaching. In that way the church got hold of a number of parish members; many of the parents also joined the Moravian Church, reasoning that if their children belonged to that church, then surely they could also. Others were more resistant. Thus the feuding began, and this was the reason there gradually came to be so many churches.

The Methodists began to assert themselves among the Germans. A Methodist minister came and worked there, and he managed to get the Germans to split off and organize a small congregation. They built a nice little church and a parsonage and got a minister from the oldest conference, so as far as that went, everything was settled. Then the Moravian Church began intensive work among the other Germans and organized a congregation which also built a church and a parsonage, and called a minister from the headquarters in Bethlehem, Pennsylvania. There were other German families who would not join either the Methodists or the Moravians, but they realized that if they stayed isolated, they would be overpowered by the other sects. So they decided to organize themselves into a Lutheran congregation, build a church, and call a properly ordained Lutheran minister, one who could truly stand up to both the Methodists and the Moravian congregation, and put them in their proper place. And they did get their German Lutheran minister. He told Per that he had come in order to see to it that no one would jump the fence. He kept his word, too, for since that time it has never been heard that any of the German Lutherans abandoned their church and went over to other sects.

There had long been talk among the Norwegians in Ephraim and the surrounding countryside about organizing a Lutheran congregation and building a church where they could follow the practices which they were accustomed to in the old country, for the Moravian service was so different that they did not really feel at home. For example, during Communion, the minister said a prayer; he then took a piece of bread himself, and gave the plate to the person beside him, with the words: "All of you, eat of this." And the plate, or the bread, went around until everyone had eaten. Likewise also with the wine. Now when all of this was over, then came the Kiss of Love. It went in this manner: each man took his neighbor by the hand, and wished him God's peace with a kiss; the women did the same thing. As far as they go, customs and ceremonies are not so important, but when people have been raised since childhood in the Norwegian Lutheran tradition, they feel like strangers when they have to take part in such unaccustomed ceremonies.

There is, likewise, the custom in the Moravian Church that all important matters are decided by the casting of lots. Yes, even marriages are arranged in that way. In Green Bay there was a young Dane, a goldsmith by profession. He got it into his head that he wanted to marry and wrote to the elders of Christiansfeldt to draw a lot for him and send a girl to be his wife. Sure enough, the girl came, but the goldsmith didn't like her and there was no wedding. But surely, if there is no belief in such a casting of lots, then it is of no use. Now, one might think that marriages conceived in this manner would make it possible for a poor person to acquire a rich wife, or that a rich man would be able to marry a poor girl. But it doesn't work that way, since the congregation's elders know how to arrange it so that such things don't happen. For whenever someone requests a wife, three girls of the same social position and financial circumstances as the petitioner are picked out; and then whoever the lot falls upon becomes the right one. The good men see to it that wealth and poverty are never united.

Then there was the time when the building sites were supposed to be apportioned to the different members of the congregation. As this was a complicated affair, it had to be decided by lot. One man from Green Bay by the name of Davidson got a rather stony piece, about which he became more than just displeased; he was extremely indignant. He said that if they didn't have anything but a rock-covered slope to give him, then they could keep it themselves, and he would go back to Green Bay, where he had come from. In the end, the minister and his assistants had to give Davidson another lot. If it really was true that God took any notice of the lot-casting or if the people believed in their hearts that it was true, then every one would have to be content with what fell to him. But the truth is that belief probably lasts as long as things fall to one's liking; in the opposite case, there is rebellion in the heart, and the entire belief is thrown overboard.

These and many other things prevented the Norwegian Lutherans from taking an interest in the Moravian Church; instead they planned to get a real Lutheran church built with a minister who both would and could administer the religious services in the manner to which they were accustomed from home. The Swedes in Sister Bay had already built a little Lutheran church (which belonged to the Augustana Synod), but there were, there as elsewhere, also defectors, since a great many of the Swedes were Baptists. Meanwhile, a Baptist lay preacher came over from Sweden and soon began to throw his net out in order to gather followers. He proved to be so successful that in the next year he was able to get a Baptist church built and a little congregation organized. Now there were, in addition to the Moravian church, five churches in a little area half as large as Holt parish. There were also, besides the Norwegians in Ephraim, many others who lived scattered and outside the different faiths and the intention was to gather them into a church community and build a church in Ephraim. (Some wanted the congregation to join the Wisconsin Synod and get a minister from them who could really take both

Methodists and Baptists, and even members of the Moravian Church, to task. Others, however, were more liberal and did not wish to belong to any synod but would rather call the church the Free Evangelical Lutheran Church, tolerating people of other persuasions and thereby avoiding all unnecessary discord.) Lists were sent out for subscriptions; some put their names down for $5.00, others for $10.00, some for $15.00, and some for $25.00. Per pledged $100. He also received $300 to $400 from the wholesale dealers in Milwaukee and Chicago with whom he had business connections; in this way about $1,000 came in for the church building.

Per was chosen to assume responsibility for the construction of the church and began to purchase materials and negotiate with a Norwegian and a Danish carpenter, who undertook the building for $300. The church was supposed to be fifty feet long, thirty feet wide, and eighteen feet high from floor to ceiling, with a choir over the entrance and a tower. When the church was finished, it had cost $1,800 with the interior furnishings, the bell in the tower, and the organ. It might seem that it was unnecessary to build another church, as there were so many already, but since the idea was to get the Lutherans together into a congregation, it was indeed necessary to have a gathering place; and as Ephraim was situated centrally, it was decided to build the church there. It was not very pleasant for the Lutherans always to be exposed to the sects' proselytizing, and this would be the case as long as they did not have a church building and a leader.

Now that the church was completed, it had to be consecrated. (Per had received a letter from a Norwegian Lutheran minister in Marinette — a town on the other side of Green Bay — in which he praised the Norwegian Lutherans of Ephraim for their sacrifice in building a church and working to preserve the Lutheran faith in an area where they were surrounded by all kinds of sects. He also said that he would be pleased to come over and preach in their new church; his hope no doubt was to be invited to dedicate the church, and thereby have it incorporated into the Norwegian Synod.) Instead Per traveled to Chicago and asked Pastor Torgersen to draft a constitution for the congregation and to give the dedication sermon, which he promised to do.[30] And in order to truly show their tolerance, they invited both the Moravian congregation's minister and, in addition, the Methodist and Baptist ministers to take part in the dedication ceremony. (Pastor Torgersen did not belong to any synod, so the ministers of the Norwegian Synod took a dim view of him, and when the Lutherans in Ephraim used him to dedicate their church and, in addition, asked the local ministers to take part in the dedication service, then there was no more sympathy to be had from the Synod ministers.)

On Sunday the 5th of August in 1880 the Lutheran Church in Ephraim was dedicated.[31] The Moravian minister first gave a prayer. Then the Baptist minister recited some passages from the Bible, whereupon Pastor Torgersen ascended the pulpit and gave the dedication sermon. The church was packed. (Some time thereafter Per wrote to the earlier mentioned minister at Marinette, asking him to come and preach in their new church, since they still did not have their own minister. The pastor answered that he was unable to come because he was wrapped up in work in his own congregation, and he further believed his coming would be of little use. For since they had dedicated the church outside of the Synod and invited ministers who were not members of the Synod — even the pastor of the Moravian Church — he could not consider them to be Lutherans. This was of course a blow to them, but they remained unperturbed. They felt themselves to be as genuinely Lutheran as the Synod people. Their constitution contained both the Nicene and the Athanasian confessions, so there was nothing lacking, and they could rightfully call themselves Lutherans. It was a major concern of the Lutherans in Ephraim to stay out of the church struggle, for it had been going on since the first Norwegian ministers came to this country. There had been an uninterrupted newspaper polemic, referred to among the common people as the "priests' squabble.")

Pastor Torgersen recommended to the congregation in Ephraim a Norwegian minister by the name of Johan Olsen

from Chicago.[32] A meeting was held in the church at which it
was decided to send a letter of call to Olsen, and offer him
$400 a year along with a free house and two holiday collec-
tions, namely Christmas and Easter. Olsen accepted the offer
and immediately moved to Ephraim. The Norwegians in
Ephraim, then, had both church and minister, and so far things
had gone well; but now the congregation had debts amounting
to $800 for the church building, and in addition, the parsonage
had to be paid for. It began to be hinted that one or another
member wanted to leave the congregation — obviously in
order to escape the debt. That could indeed have had serious
results, since the demands would then be so much greater on
those who stayed. There was danger that the whole thing
could go down the drain. To prevent that, Per declared before
the entire congregation that the church's debt was paid, and
that they would not be responsible for anything other than the
parsonage. This offer seemed to satisfy the people and there
were no withdrawals heard of after that time, but it cost Per
$800.

(The original idea was to gather all the Lutherans in
Ephraim and the surrounding area into one congregation and
then to build the church in Ephraim, which was situated in
the middle and could therefore serve as a center for all the
smaller places in the vicinity. This was reasonable, since the
distance between them was only one or two miles. However,
when Pastor Olsen began his work, he traveled to these places
preaching and setting up new congregations with various
names, so that the result was a division and a weakening of the
original congregation. Whether the minister did this in order
to earn a reputation as a founder of many congregations is not
known; but since he himself belonged to the General Synod
and incorporated these small congregations into that synod, it
is reasonable to think that this was the case.[33] In time he also
persuaded the congregation in Ephraim to join the General
Synod, which was really against its constitution. However,
this did not take place until after Per had left Ephraim; as long
as he was there things were held together, for he was looked
upon as a leader in the congregation.

(There are now two churches in Ephraim, one Lutheran and one Moravian. In the German settlement, which is situated one mile from Ephraim, there are three churches, one Lutheran, one Moravian, and one Methodist. About two miles farther north there are two churches, a Swedish Lutheran and a Swedish Baptist church. About three miles farther north there are two churches, one German and one Norwegian-Swedish, both of which are Lutheran. Thus there are now nine churches in an area about half the size of Holt parish, which would not be too large for one church, either in area or in population. But this is the way things turn out whenever the sects are allowed to spread. Then there is no end to the building of churches and founding of congregations, for people don't remember that they are few in number and therefore unable to support a church and a minister. And because this is so, there is a kind of poverty among the churches in America, particularly in the pioneer areas, where the population is small and without means. In the larger old Norwegian settlements conditions are naturally much better, with capable ministers who know how to keep people together and fend off the invasion of sects.)

For a long time Per had thought about selling out and going back to Norway to live there the rest of his days. He decided to sell his business to James, who was now without employment, and they agreed that James should buy it all, both the real estate and the movable property, for a purchase price of $10,000. The transaction was completed, and James assumed the business. Per and Mary then moved to another house which belonged to James and which Per had reserved in the arrangement for a purchase price of $500. The same house was later sold to the Lutheran congregation for the parsonage. This was in the year 1881. Two years later, in 1883, Per and Mary moved back to Norway after having lived in America for thirty-seven years.

Per and Mary are now seventy-four years old and have therefore been in America and in Norway the same amount of time, namely thirty-seven years in each place. Per bought a house on the farm Østeraa in Holt, with a little land belonging to it; in the title deed the place was given the name *Fredheim* [Peaceful home].[34] Per and Mary now live there in peace and contentment after many years of hardship both in Norway and in America: so this book ought rightly to be called *On Both Sides of the Ocean.*

> Here I'll raise my Ebenezer,
> Hither by Thy help I'm come;
> And I hope, by Thy good pleasure,
> Safely to arrive at home.
> Jesus sought me when a stranger,
> Wand'ring from the fold of God;
> He, to rescue me from danger,
> Interposed His precious blood.[35]

NOTES

[1] The croft Hagen or Haven, which lay a short distance up into the hills above the farm Ulevåg, is now completely overgrown with forest and brush-wood, and all that remains are the stone walls of a small building. A cup-sized hole in a rock between Ulevåg and Hagen is referred to as "Per Hagen's Coffee Measure." According to Henrik Mangår Ullevåg, the present owner of one of the Ulevåg farms, Per Hagen (Peter Peterson) would sometimes come down to Ulevåg to borrow coffee and he then used the hole to measure the amount.

[2] The British attack upon Copenhagen and the confiscation of the Danish-Norwegian fleet in September of 1807 drove Denmark-Norway into the arms of Napoleon. During the following seven years, when the two countries joined Napoleon's Continental system, the southern counties of Norway suffered in particular, because they depended on grain imports from Jutland. Some 1,400 Danish-Norwegian ships were confiscated and about 7,000 Norwegian and Danish seamen were confined to the hulks in Chatham and other British ports. For a brief general treatment of the period, see T. K. Derry, *A History of Scandinavia* (Minneapolis, 1979), 196–219.

[3] Peter Peterson's mother was Astrid Olsdatter, born around 1780; she was married in 1805 to the sailor Anders Aanonsen Ulevåg, who was born in 1775 and died in poverty in 1837. According to the Dypvåg church register, Peter was an illegitimate child, his real father being the local farmer and sailor Peder Hansen Størdal. Peder Hansen was born at Ulevåg in 1777 but later acquired the farm Størdal through marriage. He received the silver medal of the Royal Danish Dannebrog Order for valor shown during the war with England. The incident in question has been dramatically retold by Josef Landgraff and Constantinus Flood, both accounts being based on the records of a trial held at Sandvigen, Dypvåg, on October 5, 1810. The following is a translation of Landgraff's account in *Lidt fra gamle dage i Nedenæs* (Events from the old days in Nedenæs):

"The brig *Kolbjørnsvig*, of 58 register tons, belonging to Jacob Aall and sailing under the command of Henrik Jensen, left St. Petersburg on August 14, 1810, with a cargo of tallow, ropes, canvas, sole leather, soap, candles, horsehair, feathers, salted meat, hemp, iron, and potassium, purchased by Aall and intended for the town of Tvedestrand. On August 19, however, off the island of Hogland in the Bay of Finland, it was captured by the English frigate *Erebos* under Captain Outridge. A watch consisting of one soldier and two sailors was placed on board, and the brig remained lying here with the frigate until August 22, when the *Erebos* sailed off with the brig in tow. On September 7, off the island of Øland, the brig received a British crew consisting of one lieutenant, one soldier, one pilot, and four sailors, and was sent to Hanau, where it anchored alongside a unit of the British fleet consisting of two ships of the line, some frigates, and a number of merchant vessels.

"Of the Norwegian crew, the mate and one sailor had already been taken on board the *Erebos*; now the boatswain, one sailor, and the ship's boy were taken away, so that only the captain and the ship's carpenter, Peder Hansen Ulevåg, besides a little boy of eleven years from Tvedestrand by the name of Thor Nielsen, remained on board. The British crew was also changed. Only the soldier stayed with the brig and was joined by the eighteen-year-old cadet Thomas Harriot and four sailors. After a week the whole fleet — some 150 sails, one three-decker, one two-decker, two frigates, and a bomb ketch — set to sea with a course through the Belt. The brig was bound for Hull in England.

"However, while they were still in the harbor, the captain and the carpenter had decided they would try to take their brig back and regain liberty, even though the attempt might cost them their lives. With a rope, which they led through a hole in the wall of the crew's cabin and which in the evening they tied to their bodies, they devised a way of awakening each other and indicating when to start the attack. The captain was in the stateroom with the cadet. On October 2, the brig was in the southern end of the convoy, some nine miles south-southeast of Kristiansand. The cadet had gone to bed in the stateroom and the soldier and the two sailors lay fully dressed in the crew's quarters, while the two other Englishmen were on deck, one at the helm, the other on the watch.

"At 11:30 p.m. the carpenter gave his signal, ran up on deck, and struck the helmsman a blow which threw him overboard; then he picked up one of the two swords the helmsman had lying in front of him and with it attacked the other Englishman. The captain had immediately taken the pistol which the sleeping cadet had at his side; however, when it misfired twice and the cadet woke up, he hit him with the pistol so that he fell back into the bed. He was about to run up on deck but was met by the soldier and the two sailors, and when he tried to hit one of them with the pistol, it slipped out of his hand. The cadet had recovered consciousness and joined the others, and, as the captain bent down to pick up the weapon, all four of the Englishmen fell on top of him. At this point, however, the carpenter, who had wounded the watchman, came to the captain's aid. He thrust his sword into the soldier's thigh, the captain then got hold of the pistol, and the Englishmen fled into the stateroom, where they bolted the door. The carpenter stationed himself outside with the sword, the captain went to the skylight and threatened to shoot unless the Englishmen surrendered, and, when they refused, shot into the room to scare them and hit the soldier in the arm, whereupon one of the sailors begged for mercy. After that everyone remained quiet, while the captain went to the helm, the carpenter tended the sails, and the little boy watched for land. They managed to reach Norway near Homborsund, where they were joined by a pilot with a boat and two men, who helped anchor the brig at Hesnes. From here they sailed on, accompanied by a gun vessel and the pilot boat, and on Wednesday, October 3, at 11 a.m., they dropped anchor at Sandvigen. The English sailor [the watchman] had died of his wounds and been thrown overboard; the other four were taken prisoner and given over to the commander at Sandvigen fortress, from where the soldier was brought to a hospital. The value of the brig was estimated at $5,500 and the cargo at $40,000; the captain and the carpenter made a reasonable settlement with Aall about their reward for recapturing the ship and cargo.

"Thus two courageous men had not only salvaged valuable property for their country, but — what for them personally was more important — they had freed themselves from British captivity, which was greatly and justifiably feared, and they surely deserved the distinction that came to them in the form of the silver cross of the Royal Danish Dannebrog Order. What Flood tells us in his book *For otti aar siden* [Eighty Years Ago] in connection with this story is therefore quite surprising, that in their own town of Dybvåg there was considerable ill feeling against the two men because they, and particularly the carpenter, had practiced unnecessary cruelty." At this point, Landgraff defends the two men on the usual grounds that they risked their own lives, and that war is war. However, Constantinus Flood had actually spoken to people who remembered the incident and he only reported what he had been told. It was said, for example, that when the medals were presented by the pastor at Dypvåg church, the animosity against the two men was so intense that they wished they had not been there. See Constantinus Flood, *For otti aar siden* (Christiania, 1890); Josef Frank Caspar Landgraff, *Lidt fra gamle dage i Nedenæs* (Grimstad, 1898), 47–52; Daniel Danielsen, *Dypvåg* (Oslo, 1958), 1790–1792.

[4] At confirmation, the young men and women were ranked on the church floor according to the social standing of the parents. Peter Peterson, the son of a tenant farmer, and an illegitimate child, may have been placed far back. Bjørnstjerne Bjørnson, among others, has treated this practice in his rustic tale *En glad gut* (A Happy Boy), chapter 6. The minister at Dypvåg in the 1830s was Ole Herstad Schiøtt.

[5] Østre Risøen was formerly the name of the present town of Risør.

[6] Peter Peterson's mother, Astrid Olsdatter, died on January 8, 1845, at the age of 64.

[7] According to Henrik Mangår Ullevåg, the marsh is known today as *Wrolds myr*. Old documents use the name *Evensås*.

[8] Peter Peterson's stone fences can still be seen in the woods northeast of Ulevåg.

[9] In addition to his illegitimacy, Peter Peterson had to contend with Norwegian class distinctions, a common theme in nineteenth-century literature, from Bjørnstjerne Bjørnson's *En glad gut* (1860) to H. A. Foss' *Husmands-Gutten* (The Cotter's Boy), in 1889. Although Peter's fiancée, Kirsten Marie (1821–1904), came from one of the smaller farms at Østerå, her father, Nils Stiansen Østerå, owned his farm, like his ancestors for many generations before him, while Peter's mother and her husband were cotters and paupers. Names such as Aase Langnæb (Langnæb = long beak) are fictitious and probably represent various gossiping members of the Østerå family. On the subject of Østerå, see Sven Svensen, *Holt. En bygdebok* (Stavanger, 1940), 468.

[10] Emigration from South Norway to America was considerable around 1850. Of the 32,270 Norwegians who left Norway for America in the years 1845–1855, no less than 2,480, or 7 percent, came from Aust Agder. Two of the best known emigrants, Elise Tvede Wærenskjold and Johan Reiersen, both came from Holt, near Tvedestrand. More than any other person, Reiersen, who began publishing *Christianssandsposten* in 1839, spread the good news about America among the people of the two Agder counties. In 1844, after a tour of the United States, he wrote his *Veiviser for norske emigranter til De*

forenede nordamerikanske stater og Texas (translated as *Pathfinder for Norwegian Emigrants*). In it Reiersen praised the Norwegian settlements in Illinois and Wisconsin, though he himself favored Texas and in 1845 led an expedition there, which landed in New Orleans in June of that year. Some of the members of the group, however, continued north to Missouri and Wisconsin, and in years to come the Midwest was the goal of most emigrants from South Norway. Reasons for this change were the climate, the slavery in the South, and the fact that from the 1850s on emigration ships put in at Quebec in Canada — far from Texas, but close to the Midwest. Like many of his compatriots from Aust Agder, then, Peter Peterson originally intended to go to New Orleans, but instead settled in the Midwest. See Ingrid Semmingsen, *Agder og Amerika* (Oslo, 1953), 34–40.

[11] Desertion was common on Scandinavian ships in Great Britain, America, and Canada. From 1846 to 1850, 502 Norwegians deserted in New York, and only 25 were caught. Deserters were normally motivated by the higher wages on British and American ships or by opportunities on land; another cause was the Norwegian type of hiring contract, according to which sailors had to sign on for several years at a time. In Peter Peterson's case, the reason was simply his wish to get to America. See Jacob S. Worm-Müller, *Den norske sjøfarts historie*, 2 (Oslo, 1935), 579–580.

[12] The famous first Thames tunnel was built by Sir Marc Isambard Brunel (1769–1849) in the Rotherhithe-Wapping area. Begun in 1825, it was completed in 1843.

[13] Liverpool must be New Liverpool, situated near St. Romuald.

[14] St. Nicholas, on the St. Lawrence, lies approximately fifteen miles west of Quebec.

[15] New Ireland, near St. Ferdinand, is sixty miles south-southeast of Quebec.

[16] Several letters from Norwegians in Wisconsin (Ansten Nattestad, Søren Bache, Anders Wiig, Hans Christian Brandt) were published in Norwegian newspapers in the 1840s and helped build up the reputation of Wisconsin as the best place for Norwegians. See Theodore Blegen, *Land of Their Choice* (Minneapolis, 1955), 267–279.

[17] Ole Larsen later moved to Wisconsin and in 1852 bought Eagle Island in Door county. He mentioned to a group of Norwegian Moravians in Fort Howard (Green Bay) that government lands were available around Eagle Harbor, where, in 1853, the Moravians settled and founded the town of Ephraim. Here Peter Peterson later established his business. See John Kahlert, *Pioneer Cemeteries. Door County, Wisconsin* (Bailey's Harbor, Wisconsin, 1981), 163–166.

[18] Indian Land: Norwegian settlers referred to the region around Iola, Waupaca county, Wisconsin, as "Indilandet."

[19] This story is also told by the child's older brother, Fritz William Rasmussen, in his memoirs.

[20] The history of the founding of New Denmark has been told by Fritz Rasmussen; in addition, the Rasmussen papers contain a long letter from F. R. Hiorth about its settlement. The letters of Andreas Frederiksen to his family in Denmark also tell about the early years at New Denmark. One of Frederiksen's letters, in which Peter Peterson is mentioned, has been translated by Kristian Hvidt in his *Danes Go West* (Skørping, 1976), 71. In addition, several references to Cooperstown (New Denmark) are contained in A. M. Iverson's unpublished memoirs.

[21] The two brothers Halvor (b. 1822) and Aslak (b. 1829) Andersen from Ulevåg were the sons of Anders Halvorsen Ulevåg, who owned a farm close to the croft Hagen on which Peter Peterson grew up. Aslak Andersen moved to

Ephraim, where he later became a prosperous farmer and businessman. He died in 1892. See Hjalmar Ruud Holand, *History of Door County*, 2 (Chicago, 1917), 98–103.

[22] According to Fritz Rasmussen, Casper Hansen (and Peter Peterson before him) owned the northwest quarter of the southwest quarter of section 26 in what is now known as New Denmark (T 22 N-R 22 E). Niels Godtfredsen owned the northwest quarter of section 26.

[23] James Hanson (Jens Hansen) was born in August of 1852. In 1875 he married Olive (Olava) Helgeson. He was the postmaster and a prosperous businessman in Ephraim, gifted with a sense of humor and well liked by his neighbors. He died in June, 1916. A granddaughter, Olive Smith, still lives in Ephraim. Hanson's obituary was printed in *The Door County Democrat*, June 9, 1916.

[24] Andreas Michael Iverson was born in Kristiansand in 1823. He attended the newly established missionary school in Stavanger from 1844 to 1849 and in 1849 came to Milwaukee as pastor for a group of Scandinavian Moravians. In May of 1850 he was ordained by Bishop Van Vleck at Bethlehem, Pennsylvania, and later the same year moved with his congregation to a colony founded by Nils Otto Tank near Green Bay, Wisconsin. At this time he also established his first contact with the settlers at Cooperstown, whom he visited regularly during the following years. In March of 1851, because of a conflict with Tank over property rights, Iverson and the Moravian colonists moved to Fort Howard, but after receiving a loan of $500 from Bethlehem in the spring of 1853, they traveled north to settle the area later known as Ephraim. Iverson also established Moravian churches in Sturgeon Bay and later in Green Bay. In 1883 he was removed from the church after being convicted of "gross moral delinquency" (a sexual relationship with a 17-year-old member of his congregation); he then studied for a year in Chicago and afterward practiced medicine in Green Bay and Sturgeon Bay until his death in 1907. Iverson originally looked upon Per Hagen as a friend, but after Per began his work to establish a Lutheran church, Iverson considered him his chief enemy in Ephraim. In the 1890s, A. M. Iverson wrote a history of the Scandinavian Moravian Church in Wisconsin. It was translated into English by John Boler in 1929 as "A Brief Account of the Activity of the Evangelical Brethren Congregation among the Scandinavians in Wisconsin," but neither the Norwegian original (in Ephraim Moravian Church) nor the translation (at the Wisconsin State Historical Society) has been published. See *Dictionary of Wisconsin Biography* (Madison, 1960), 187, and Kahlert, *Pioneer Cemeteries*, 157–161.

[25] The Lutheran minister belonging "to a contentious party" was probably Ludvig Marinus Biørn (1835–1908), who served as pastor at Manitowoc from 1861 to 1879.

[26] In his history of the Moravian Church, Iverson recalls how, in the late 1850s, Peter Peterson and his friend Aslak Andersen bought 150 acres of the Ephraim lakefront, promising "during the coming winter to build for us a large and serviceable pier, from which vessels could take their cargoes and on which all our people could place all their cordwood and fence posts to be sold without any charge being made" (Iverson, "A Brief Account," 105). Per's wharf from the early seventies, then, must have been a second pier. In his letter to a friend in Norway in 1875 he mentions that Ephraim has two piers.

[27] Hans Gundersen's pastor was the renowned G. A. Lammers, who served as minister at Bamble from 1836 to 1848. Later he moved to Skien, where Ibsen's mother and sister came under his influence. Orator, artist, politician, he is generally taken to be the model for Ibsen's character Brand.

[28] The quotation is from Ivar Aasen's poem "Upp og ned" (Up and down),

the second stanza. The poem was first published in 1881, long after Per
Hagen's visit to Norway. Aasen's text:
> Du kjem til ein Gard, der du tyktest vera kjend,
> du gled deg til aa finna den gamle gode Grend.
> Men Grendi er snudd um; du finn aldri det du vil,
> dei gamle Folk er burte, og ny'er komne til.

[29] The poem is the first stanza of Ivar Aasen's "Dei gamle Fjelli" from the
collection *Symra* (1863). Both Aasen poems here were translated by Harald
Naess. Aasen's text:
> Dei gamle Fjell i Syningom
> er alltid eins aa sjaa,
> med same gamle Bryningom
> og same Toppom paa.
> I Bygdom byggja Sveinarne,
> og Huset stender laust;
> men dei gamle Merkesteinarne
> dei standa lika traust.

[30] John Zacharias Torgerson (1841–1905) was born in Bergen, Norway. He
belonged to the Eielsen Synod and served as president of the Hauge College
and Eielsen Seminary in Chicago. After 1876 he left the synod and helped to
found the German Evangelical Lutheran Seminary in Chicago. Torgerson is
said to have "visited 15,000 homes and married 15,000 couples."

[31] According to O. M. Norlie in *Norske lutherske menigheter i Amerika*, 1
(Minneapolis, 1918), 287, the congregation known as Bethania Menighet, in
Door county, Wisconsin, was organized in 1882 and in 1897 joined the United
Church. At that time it had 119 members, but in 1915 only 46. A more detailed
account is given in the pamphlet *Seventy-Fifth Anniversary of Bethany
Lutheran Church, Ephraim, Wisconsin. 1882–1957*, which supplies the following information: "Peter Peterson, a prominent merchant and dock-owner
with the faith of Noah, was determined that the landmark he had cherished
since childhood should be set in Ephraim. Being a merchant and dock-owner
he was acquainted with many captains of sailing vessels. With Mr. Peterson
contacting Pastor Biorn, it was made possible for Pastor Biorn to come to
Ephraim occasionally and conduct services which were usually held in the
homes of Peter Peterson, Morton Olson and Thomas Goodletson. . . . By
October 23, 1882 the building was completed at a total cost of $1,569.14 of
which $825.66 had been obtained. To complete the payment Mr. Peter Peter-
son contributed a sum of $743.48. . . . A constitution for the Scandinavian
Free Evangelical Lutheran Congregation of Ephraim, Door county, Wisconsin, written in twelve articles, was accepted by the members at the organ-
izational meeting on March 31st, 1882 . . . In 1883 the parsonage was purchased for $800 but Mr. Peterson knew it would be a great hardship for the
Congregation to pay that amount. Mr. Peterson was now living in Norway. He
notified Mr. James Hanson, his attorney [sic], to deed the parsonage and the
lot to the congregation. . . . In 1895 the congregation was united with the
Augustana Synod. . . . On January 4th, 1898 . . . the congregation affiliated
itself officially with the United Lutheran Church of America. . . . The years
1897–1910 were good years for the congregation. The membership steadily
increased until the latter year when the State of Wisconsin bought up home-
steads [in what is now Peninsula State Park]. Twelve families were lost to
Bethania Congregation in this transfer."

[32] O. M. Norlie, in *Who's Who Among Pastors in All the Norwegian Lutheran Synods of America* (Minneapolis, 1928), 434, lists him as Johannes Olsen
(1844–1921). The *Seventy-Fifth Anniversary* pamphlet mentioned above de-

scribes him as a gifted musician, poet, and writer, who ended his days as postmaster at Pemberton, Minnesota.

[33] Johan Olsen left Ephraim in 1892 and in the following years served congregations in Illinois (1892–1895), Michigan (1897–1903), and Minnesota (1903–1910), all of which belonged to the United Church.

[34] Letters written by Peter and Marie Peterson to James and Olive Hanson in Ephraim tell of their last years. Marie seems to have had some difficulty readjusting to Norway. Peter Peterson continued to discuss financial matters with his foster son — advising him to treat his debtors with patience and understanding. He also composed the present memoir and in 1898 wrote his will, according to which 4,000 Norwegian *kroner* were given to various friends and the house *Fredheim* to Kirsten Severine Eldrup, a distant relative of Marie who helped the old couple in the house. After Kirsten Eldrup died in 1910 *Fredheim* was owned by her sister, Nicoline (Eldrup) Henriksen. Since 1965 it has belonged to Nicoline's daughter, Solveig Dalen. Solveig Dalen (b. 1905) writes that she remembers her mother quoting Peter Peterson: "Du blir aldri fattig av det du gir bort." (You never get poor from what you give away.) Peter Peterson died on January 10, 1900. Marie died in 1904.

[35] The stanza, quoted in English by Peterson, is the second verse of the hymn "Come Thou Fount of Every Blessing," by Robert Robinson (1735–1790). According to the Reverend Warren Sautebin, Madison, Wisconsin, the line "Here I'll Raise my Ebenezer" was earlier used in the Moravian liturgy.